FACT OR FICTION

You Couldn't Make This Shit Up!

By

C.A.Scrimshaw

PREFACE:

I have always wanted to tell my story, not for sympathy or to shock anyone but to show I am human, my life has been far from perfect but I suppose it is so much of the bad that brings out the good in me. I feel things but I don't always show it. I'm not hard but I'm not naive either

It's not one of those broken child books. I am and never will be broken. I am a strong woman with a successful career. I don't believe being abused makes people abuse others, that is an excuse. I know I didn't like what happened to me so why would I go on and do that to someone else?

I waited until my mum passed away to write this as I never wanted her to know the truth, she has had enough hurt in her life.

Why is it called fact or fiction? sometimes I have said to myself " You couldn't make this shit up" but then wonder if people would actually believe me if I told them. I really don't care if you believe it, I know it is true and I hope if it gives one girl the confidence to speak out, it was worth writing

DEDICATIONS:

Many people over my life have told me I should write a book, so here it is, I dedicate this to them.

To Jane for being the one person I felt strong enough to confide in and for giving me the courage to change my life for the better

To Angela, one of my oldest friends who without her help, financially, physically and emotionally I would probably never be where I am today.

To my children who have struggled sometimes by the life choices I made, and have shown me that no matter how your life starts out it is up to you how you live it.

To Nigel, my best friend , my soul mate and my happy ever after (*even though I know he won't even bother reading the book*)

CHAPTER ONE: ME AND MY FAMILY

I don't want to bore you by going into too much detail ,but give you an idea of the family dynamics and how this changed over the years.

I was born in Bradford, West Yorkshire in June 1962. The youngest of six children, we lived in a 3-bedroom house on Buttershaw Estate (*"Rita, Sue and Bob Too" territory, in fact I was best friends with Andrea Dunbar's cousin at one time*) The first few years of my life were happy as I can recall.

I know loved my dad although I don't really remember that much about him. When I was very small, I remember he made up silly rhymes, one in particular about my brother sticks in my mind.

"Michael's got 'em

Pimples on his bottom"

He would sing laughing as he jigged my brother up and down on his knee to the rhythm. It would make me chuckle... I am sure he sang songs about me too but oddly enough I don't remember any, that may be a good thing.

I remember Dad buying my first proper vinyl record, "How Much is that doggy in the Window" I must have listened to it a lot because I can still remember the words !

When I was still in primary school my dad died of Cor Pulmonale. (*Heart disease that was caused secondary to lung disease.*) I remember he had a bed made up in the living room for a while because he could not manage to walk upstairs. He had been a roofer and I can't be sure but my guess is he had asbestosis long before it was a thing. He was only 39 when he died.

The last thing I remember about my dad is when he was in St Luke's hospital, Children at that time were only allowed to visit for a short time (or that is what Mum said). We were taking it in turns to go to his bedside. I was there with Michael, my brother, at this visit. Dad looked so pale and quiet in the hospital bed. There were some rather large grapes on his bedside table, he offered us one telling me to be careful because they had pips in, I reminded him I was 6 and a big girl now so he didn't have to worry. I don't think there was ever a mention of cutting them lengthways in those days, nor had I ever heard of anyone choking on the grape itself, just the pips or so my dad said anyway. I still think of my dad every time I eat fat grapes

My brother and I were then sent out onto the grass verge for the rest of visiting time and I don't remember seeing my dad again. He died that year taking with him all my sense of security. So many times, in my life I have wished my dad was still there, and how my life may have been so different if he hadn't died when he did.

My dad with me and Joyce on holiday in Heysham

I shared a room with My mum, my two sisters shared a room until Cynthia got married and then Joyce got the room to herself, my three brothers all shared a room, until David built himself a bedroom by adding a partition wall in the dining room downstairs.

My mum was a hard-working woman, she was now widowed for the second time. I was six and my brother Michael was seven. We also had 2 older sisters and two older brothers from my Mum's first marriage, her first husband also died young leaving mum a widow with 4 children but until I was an adult, I never really knew them as anything but older siblings. I still don't consider them anything other than that really, because we were never treated any different from each other (although they may all state, I was the favorite).

I believe we were a close knit and well-balanced family, with equal parts of love and fights. We looked after each other and from an early age we took turns at cooking tea and helping out when mum was at work. Some of us were better than others.

I remember Dennis cooking chips once full of 'scabs' , when we complained he just said " shut up moaning, you would eat them if you were blind !"

As I got older, I would help mum and learnt a lot of baking and cooking skills from her, and the old faithful Bero book. I got good at making my famous "slop pie". I could make a nice short crust pastry and I basically put anything I could find in the bottom of a Pyrex and covered it with pastry : A layer of corned beef or tinned hot dogs, a layer of tinned carrots, tinned potatoes and baked beans were just a few of the 'recipes' , chuck in an oxo cube and everything tasted good. I have progressed a lot since then.

My mum was practically perfect...yes really. She was the glue that held the family together. we didn't get everything we wanted as kids but we never went without food, clothes, warmth or Love. She made homecooked meals and taught us to be self-sufficient, even the boys.

On the street we lived on many of the other parents didn't work, I suppose it wasn't really common then for women to go to work, especially if they had husbands bringing in a decent wage. The other women would make fun of mum going to work as they sat on the wall gossiping and basking in the sun. I resented her in the early years because many of my friends went away on holiday without their parents in the summer holidays compliments of the Cinderella club, this was a local charity which gave seaside holidays to those underprivileged children. Because mum worked, we weren't eligible, although she told me later that my two sisters had been once and hated it, so maybe she did me a favour. Those claiming benefits also got clothing and uniform vouchers so always got new school uniform, most of mine were handed down or second hand.

Our house backed onto a playing field, the grass was always kept tidy and it was great for playing rounders or practicing gymnastic. When we played rounders, the whole street would join in, even some of the adults. Picking members of the teams one by one, I was often one of the last to be picked but I didn't care.

We played out until it got dark, sometimes we were still out after the street lights came on but you daren't go inside for anything because then mum would hear you and shout " It is dark now go get your brother it's time to come in " Sneaking in for a pee was hard ,but you could go into the kitchen by the back door and sneak a snack like a brown sauce sandwich if you were quiet.

The boys would build go carts from old abandoned prams and we would ride down the mill path , a steep driveway at the other side of the field. There was a huge wire mesh gate at the bottom and if you sat at the front of the go cart you were pretty much the brake. I hit that gate more than once.

In the summer a group of us would hang out, we would make a packed lunch, a bottle of water or juice , a few butter or jam sandwiches and disappear on our bikes for the day. Mostly around the fields towards Halifax or Queensbury.

On hot days we would spend the Day at the Lido swimming pool in Lister Park in Manningham, coming out when it started to get chilly and going into the café for chunky soup and roll because that was the cheapest thing on the menu. We would go into Cartwright Hall and I would be amazed by the costumes and creeped out by the glass cases full of bad Taxidermy, squirrels with bog eyes and birds with half the feathers missing. Nobody caused a problem or misbehaved because they knew they would get a clip round the ear and thrown out.

There is no way you would tell your parents you had been punished because they would give you a clip round the ear too.   Kids were mostly brought up to respect their elders anyway.

Family holidays were low budget but fun, we used to rent a house in Heysham, a small seaside town near Morecambe. It had all the self-catering facilities we needed, a large garden that backed onto the church yard, Me and Mick would climb the wall and get crab apples from a tree at the back, then on the first day we would be moaning about belly ache. The house was a short walk from the beach. I remember mum would get up early each morning and walk to the local shop for a newspaper, most days I would get up and go with her, I loved this little walk, just the two of us putting the world to rights without a care in the world.

The 'Hold The ball pose' in the garden at Heysham

We would have holiday spending money made up from savings, donations from family and some from mum. Each day we would budget an amount for the day and each day we would overspend and the rest of the days allowance went down, more often than not the last day is penniless. (*I still do this now when I go on holiday but try not to get down to nothing !*) We knew when it was gone, it was gone though, and no amount of whinging or begging would magic up extra spending money.

Every spring we would get new clothes for our holidays, I loved the Pretty cotton dresses , pure white knee length socks and leather T bar sandals.

Mum would always end up buying a cheap plastic mac while we were there because you could guarantee it would rain for most of the week, that was usually on the day we chose to go on the bus into Morecambe for the day. We would be dodging in and out of the gift   shops to keep warm and dry. Although the cheap plastic mac would make me sweat so much, I would probably have kept drier without a coat ! I don't remember spending time in the amusements then but I guess with 6 kids that would be pretty expensive, but we enjoyed walks into the village and to the beach. A visit to Happy Mount Park was always a must too, sometimes we went later in the evening so we could see it lit up.

The village was well known for producing nettle beer, a non-alcoholic drink believed to be some kind of tonic, made with herbs, yeast, lemons and nettles. Some believed it helped with rheumatism and some even believed it could restore hair-loss. They sold it on the main street on the outdoor market stall, it tasted rank, like dirty bath water...an acquired taste I am told. I think they still make it if you wanted to try it for yourself. (This isn't a recommendation BTW so don't come back at me if you don't like it !).

There were some huge weighing chair scales in the main street too but I don't think I ever tried them. I loved walking around the little stalls, looking at trinkets and unusual artifacts.

Mick and I would walk to Heysham head, I think it was a kind of holiday village nearby, they had rides and swings etc. You could also get a land train too and sometimes we would take a ride there

They had one of those big moon walk domes, an early version of the bouncy castles we have today, and we loved it, we would save money each day to go in there and bounce of some energy, I loved the kind of echo inside . One day we went and it was closed, some drunk guys had been in and had a fight. The guy said it was covered in blood but if we cleaned it, we could go in for free for the rest of our holiday … I felt like I was working for a forensic team, so cool lol.

I hate when I see stereotyping on TV and media, even on recent nursing study days, that portray large families as spongers and unkempt. I have even heard work colleagues make statements referring to large families. The worst is when they count the children and say things like "All those kids, two different dads and she is with someone else now!" …REALLY ? Some people need to stop seeing the world in black and white and open up their mind to a bigger picture.

I am not saying there aren't families like that but there are also small families and single parents who abuse the system just the same.

My mum worked every day of her life to keep our family together, she always said " I chose to have a big family so it is up to me to keep them, not the state". Mum instilled a great work ethic in each and every one of us. She never forced us into anything and supported us in our choices, she ended up with six hardworking Adults who followed career paths not just jobs. None of us claimed benefits in favour of a hard day's work, regardless of financial gain.

My mum always told me to never go to bed on an argument and I still keep to that rule even now. Even after the greatest blow out at my mum, I would come down and apologise before going to bed and share a hug. My mum has always been my best friend and confident and I shared everything with her, well almost everything.

Let me introduce my family : My eldest sister,

Cynthia was a legal secretary, I don't remember her being at home as she married her childhood sweetheart, Robin, when I was quite young, Robin was an Ice cream man and they had a son, Robin-john who I did babysit for in my teenage years, I was told I could help myself to ice lollies but the generator wasn't on so I wouldn't be able to have the ice cream, it was the whipped type that you pull like a pint. One evening Robin-John wanted an ice cream he told me the generator was on so it was fine, he was eight years old and like an idiot I believed him, He told me how to do it so I figured why not ? I will tell you why not, that stuff is messy when it isn't switched on, it exploded all over the ice cream van. I panicked and made him swear not to tell his dad, I spent the whole evening cleaning it only for Robin- John to tell his parents the second they came through the door !

Robin thought it was funny and said he would teach me how to do it properly. When I was at upper school, I used to help him in the summer months, sitting in the back of the ice cream van eating the fudge bars as he drove around the estate

I would go to their house sometimes for lunch from school calling in the chippy on the way.

Sadly, Cynthia was widowed when her husband Robin was only 42, it seems to me all the men in the family die young.

Cynthia also struggled with tenosynovitis in her wrists, she found it hard to type so gave up secretarial work after many years. She moved to Bridlington later with her new boyfriend and ran a cafe for a few years until she retired and then moved back to Bradford. She always seemed to be the cool sister, the one who wore make up, fashionable clothes and had a social life. She left home when I was still quite young so was never really much of an influence to me as I was growing up.

David, my Eldest Brother was a Master butcher. He became a father figure after my dad died until he left home and got married. David married Jean, who he met at work and they both worked hard until retirement age. They would have made great parents but by the time they decided to try for a family things did not go to plan, also at that time it was very difficult to adopt a baby when you were older, the options were usually a disabled or older child. My kids loved him when they were younger, he was a great uncle to them. He always seemed to get them the best Christmas gifts too which was a bonus.

I remember at age 13 when Mum discovered I was smoking and allowed me to smoke at home "Better at home than on the street "she would say. I was not so open to share my habit with David though and it was a while before he caught me smoking, he gave me a right telling off even though I told him mum knew and even bought my cigs!

David was very protective; he gave me the 'stranger danger' talk and right after I was walking from the shops and a voice out of a car shouted "Hey little girl does you want a ride?" I shouted "FUCK OFF!" and ran away. When I got home it turned out that it had been my brother with some of his mates in the car, I was sure he was gonna kill me for swearing but instead he congratulated me on using my head.

According to mum it was David who got me my first bike, I am not sure where he got it but it was an old bike and he painted it and renovated it for me and I loved it !

I tried to ride Mick's bike once, it was a boys bike so had the crossbar, I had to climb on a wall to get on it. As I rode down the street, I realised my feet didn't touch the floor and had no idea of how to stop it. I crashed into a parked ice cream van at the end of the street and landed on the crossbar. It hurt so much and I started to bleed. I just shoved tissue in my knickers and daren't tell anyone as I should not have been on the bike in the first place and was afraid to get into trouble.

On a recent study day for child protection, they talked about delayed presentation being a red flag and I thought back to how mum could have got into a lot of trouble if it had not healed or I got an infection and she was totally oblivious to it.

My other Sister Joyce was a Librarian, she still worked in the library after retirement age and also as a classroom assistant. She is responsible for my love of books. When studying to be a nurse and the tutors would tell you to put notes in the margin ...WTF ??? NOOOOO ! Use a post it note if you must or better still buy yourself a notebook ! (I wonder how many of my readers are holding a hi-lighter as they are reading this ...PUT IT DOWN !!!)

I remember when Joyce was younger, she worked on a book stall in Kirkgate market too, she would bring me little books home: colouring books and magic painting books with the sheet of tracing paper between pages. I especially liked the dress up doll books, cute little cherubic paper dolls with an assortment of frilly dresses, each with the little tabs you fold over to stop them falling off.

I guess you could say Joyce is the serious one, not the kind of sister I would have sneaked in her room to steal clothes and makeup, although I do remember going in her room to watch Top of the Pops on her black and white TV. If I am 100% honest, I couldn't wait for her to move out so I could have her room.

Joyce is married to Tony and has two children: Marisa and Frankie, her eldest Marisa I was always particularly close to because I looked after her when she was a baby, I would treat her the same as my own, including discipline and mealtimes. A very fussy eater for her mum but always ate what I gave her. Joyce once said I could serve her sheep's eyeballs and she would eat them ha-ha. I'm not sure if it is because I am a better cook or she was just afraid of starving to death when I gave her food to the dog . I never offered an alternative lol. Marisa was particularly close to my son Daniel as they grew up together and had similar interests.

My brother Dennis has had various jobs from long distance lorry driver to driving instructor, I have often heard him describe himself as the black sheep of the family, but I disagree, maybe he doesn't go out drinking with David and Mick, but I am pretty sure he is loved by us all. I have always found him to be there for me and I suppose over the years he has been the one who keeps in touch the most. Dennis was the one who picked me up from school when mum was working and I loved to tease him telling him Chelsea was better than Man United when I had never even watched a football match in my life!

At the worst time of my life Dennis was there for me, he was engaged to Angela at the time and they had a house together, they would let me stay there at weekends and often took me out with them for the day. Angela became a very close friend and still someone I consider as part of the family long after her and Dennis split up. The split was pretty amicable so there has never been a problem having both around at family gatherings.

Dennis also has a daughter , Amy, so when the kids were younger, they were all pretty close , I guess having all those cousins together and all under 5 made it inevitable. They always got together for birthday parties.

Michael worked for the council, now retired, he started as a builder's labourer when he left school and worked his way up from there, ended up being a quantity surveyor and was probably earning more than I ever did ! There is only a year and 8 days between me and Michael, him being older than me. I suppose as kids we fought the most but God help anyone else who tried to hurt me because he would be there to defend me.

Michael and I were in the same class at junior school as they were two years joined together. I remember when I was in hospital, he asked the teachers for homework for me and brought it when he came to visit. Mum went mad sending him outside to collect conkers. Needless to say, I never did it!

I was somewhat of a groupie of his in my teens as he worked as a DJ in the local pubs and it meant even if I had no one to go out with I could just rock up and sit with his girlfriend of the time. Mick wouldn't think twice in humiliating us though, as we got up to dance, he would announce " Hey up, the strippers are here "

One time he was hosting a quiz in the pub. He asked "Who is this to win a pint" and played 'No Milk Today' by Herman's Hermits , I got it straight away but instead of a pint he said " No you can't win you know the answer "

No shit ! "Anyone who gets it right knows the answer ya twat !"

Michael was married to Janet, now divorced, and they have two girls Nicola and Rebecca, they would stay over sometimes at the weekend, I would borrow Rebecca to sort out Daniel's local Bullies sometimes.

So, there you are, this is my Family. As we have grown older, we have lived apart often but always came back for Mum's Christmas party on Christmas eve. A tradition going back to our childhood, but as kids we were never invited, we would all stay in one room and choose an annual to read in bed and have the TV to watch Morecambe and Wise Christmas special. As we got older, we were able to go to the party and as the family grew the grandchildren came too.

David would dress up as Santa and give out the presents from Aunties and Uncles and Mum.

The kids loved it; he was called "Uncle David Clause" by my kids. Obviously, the gifts from 'real Santa' were under the tree in the morning as usual.

Uncle David Claus with my boys

I'm not sure Christmas will ever be the same again now she is not around, already I can see cracks forming in the family cement. I used to think it was rubbish when people said once the Matriarch goes a family is never the same but now, I see what they mean.

Social media can be a bitch too, it shows you

history from years before with photos of mum and family that remind you how much you miss her, some bring a smile and some bring a tear. She was and always will be my best friend.

Chapter Two: Nobody is perfect

I was born with a dislocated hip, often referred to these days as a 'clicky hip'. at that time people did not have tests for it at birth and so nothing was done about it.

My Nanny , Frances, noticed the problem first when I was about 3, this was the lady who looked after me when mum went to work (not my grandma, but an older friend of mum's). She told mum I walked funny and asked if she minded if she got it checked out at the clinic.

I was referred to see Mr. Wishart, an Orthopaedic consultant. It was confirmed that I had not formed a hip socket and needed surgery to correct it. During my childhood I had a series of three operations. (Mr. Wishart was my hero). I told the consultant I wanted to be a ballet dancer or a nurse, he recommended nursing as he figured I might have trouble with balance if dancing, he wasn't wrong there.

During an appointment near Christmas Mr. Wishart gave me a Cherry Aime's Girls annual with the picture of a nurse on the front, I loved it, I still have it and cherish it. I was convinced he bought it especially for me but it was probably second hand and donated.

I would visit him at the Children's Hospital in Bradford, I used to love going there, it had a huge dolls house and wooden rocking horse in the waiting room, I often wonder how many thousands of children have ridden on that same horse.

The last operation was when I was 11 years old, it was at Woodlands Orthopaedic hospital in Rawdon. I was there for over three months and Visitors on the children's ward were only allowed to visit in the afternoons. The bus only came from Bradford in the afternoon on Wednesdays and Sundays so that was when mum came to visit. I used to get so upset when she went home. As a paediatric nurse I think how much more support parents and children get during their hospital stay nowadays.

On the day of my operation My mum had a telephone call telling her I had lost a lot of blood and needed a blood transfusion, they told her I had a 50/50 chance of survival. What kind of statement is that to give to a mother over the phone, miles away, with no money and no means of getting to the hospital???? My Eldest sister, Cynthia and my mum walked 9 miles to the hospital to see me, I remember waking and seeing them there, Coronation Street was on TV, I was so confused because it was only on in the evening and there was no visiting at that time. My mum was crying, although she tried to hide it, she must have been terrified. I loved the smell of home mixed with stale tobacco that would linger on her coat and would take a deep breath as she hugged me to go home. I guess I was making memories because when I am sad, I can think about that smell and it comes back...weird!

I was in a cast that encased my torso and both my legs, the left leg full length and the right to the knee, it had a hole cut out right around to my bottom to enable me to go to the toilet. I was nursed on a kind of wooden frame on my back, this was to enable them to slide a bedpan underneath without lifting me and to keep my bottom off the bed as it got pretty sore. It had grooves in to stop me rolling over but that was no deterrent I would shuffle to the edge and flip myself over, it's a wonder I didn't fall off the bed.

I wasn't alone, the other girls on the ward were good company and most of the time they were older and would look out for me.

The nurses would lay me on my tummy to

give my bottom a rest and often I would fall asleep. One day I fell asleep and the hospital teacher came in, she had been talking to me and when I didn't answer she started to shout at me. I woke with a start, she was convinced I was faking and gave me 100 lines , imagine getting lines in hospital. I told her I wasn't doing them because I was asleep. The other girls told her I was asleep and if she didn't leave me alone, they would go on strike. She wasn't happy but said " fine" and left me alone.

Woodland's hospital was every bit as beautiful as it sounds, the ward was round with huge opening doors all around the ward. The nurses would wheel the beds outside sometimes to give us fresh air and we could watch the birds and squirrels. some days it looked like something out of a Disney movie as birds flew in the ward and squirrels would come looking for titbits under the beds.

I loved hospital food too, fish and chip day was my favourite. The nurses would joke around at mealtimes and make up random stuff...at least I hope it was random " do you want beef burger or octopus?" oddly enough that octopus looked suspiciously like a burger. All mobile children were sat at the table for meals and once I was out of the cast, I would help set the table with cutlery and a cotton placemat at each place, they were pure white with double stripes down each side, when I see tea towels like that, I get a pang of nostalgia.

I loved helping them out, rolling bandages (In those days they were washed and reused not thrown away) making beds and talking to the little ones through the cot bars. There was one little one on Gallows traction, tied up by his feet spinning around the cot. I thought at the time it looked like some kind of torture but now know it is a treatment for a broken femur in a young child. I do understand though when parents are freaked out seeing me tie their little ones up in that way, it seems so barbaric.

I would sit with the baby on traction and read a story or play for a while. There were no bedside TV's and no parents so all the children would play together and look out for each other.

I had a gold cross and chain which my grandma gave me and I was wearing it when they took me down to theatre. The nurse took it off and said she would put it safe for me and winked, I never saw it again. When I asked for it, I was told she put it in my jigsaw box but someone must have taken it. I was really sad because my grandma made me promise to take good care of it.

Anyway, as you can see, I survived, but I still walk funny. I didn't even know what a limp was. One of my cousins once asked why I walked with a limp and I had to ask my mum ha-ha

I wore glasses like jam jar bottoms, they didn't thin the lenses then on NHS glasses, I had a squint / lazy eye when I was younger and had to wear a patch over my glasses for short periods. I am short sighted but the vision in my left eye is so bad I can just about see the E on the board ...but then can I see it or is it a guess? We all know the board starts with an E. My glasses were standard NHS glasses so not much of a fashion statement. It was unheard of for children to take days off school for anything then so even after a visit to the optician and having drops in my eyes I was sent back to school with a strange vision that made everything on the blackboard look like stars.

I was called specky four eyes, bog eyed, Leonard (the cross-eyed lion) among other things.

And the E.A.R yes, the Dumbo reference is there. I have odd Ears, not so noticeable now but at the time the difference was huge, my right ear sticks out and is floppy and my left ear appears normal.

Apparently, I passed this trait onto my granddaughter, Sorry!

So, Dumbo, bat ears, big ears etc. went together with being asked if I can fly or told to be careful, I don't take off with the wind.

I wet the bed well into my teens, now this may have been a symptom of other things but we will get to that later. I had regular baths but can't help wondering if I stank of Piss all the time.

My mum took me to a bed wetting clinic and they gave us a buzzing alert. It consisted of a plastic sheet that fit under my bedsheet in theory it buzzed when I needed to wee and then I would go to the toilet, a bit like Pavlov's dogs ha-ha. In practice it buzzed every time I wet it and this meant several changes a night instead of one, waking up the whole household in the process. Everyone started to complain so that was soon abandoned. They gave me little blue pills, I have no idea what they were, to take but they didn't do anything either.

This bed wetting stopped me from going on holiday with others, going on school residential trips or sleeping over at friends (*although I remember staying with one friend because when I told her she said not to worry if I wet the bed, she would blame her sister*).

It even stopped me from leaving home to live in the nursing residence because I was afraid someone would find out.

Being in the school playground with my brother singing the rainbow theme referring to my wet bed didn't help my self-esteem much but what are siblings for if not to take the Michael (literally ha-ha)

And so that was my childhood, a Bullies dream, a limp, a squint, specs, big ears and stinking of piss. I took the name calling with a pinch of salt, I never let them get to me, I suppose I didn't have the strength to fight them all so easier to ignore them

"Sticks and stones may break my bones but names will never hurt me" became a daily mantra

Being the youngest of six helped too, we constantly ragged at each other, someone was always the 'victim' in our house but ignored it goes away. the only time it was a problem was if we got physical, but mum would say " you asked for it" or " stop fighting" and all was at peace with the world, she never resorted to violence herself so we respected her word, oh except one time I nicked the chocolates out of a family hamper she had stashed for Christmas and she found out, she hit out at me but missed ,I laughed, but the second time she made BIG contact, I only ever laughed the once ....

Michael had a phrase he would use when we were both stood in front of mum with the whodunnit stare, he would say "We know who did it don't we? "…. yeah, it was usually him!

I had friends at home and school but it was also very common with girls to 'mug off' with someone else at regular intervals, during these periods they told the others your faults and then would use these against you. In these cases, it did hurt because these were people you trusted, don't get me wrong I was no angel and often fell into this category myself ...usually when my friends had 'mugged off' with someone else.

I remember my best friend at the time, Linda palling up with someone else, we weren't talking to each other but then she called for me and asked me to go for a walk, as we got around the corner the other girl beat me up. I posted a letter through her letter box with a daddy long legs in... that showed her lol.

We made up nasty rhymes about each other

" *Hop along, skip along, jump, jump, jump*" they

sang

    " *Ipsy pipsy, your mum's a gypsy*" I would sing
back

    If I told my mum she would put her arm
around me and say " Just ignore them" and I did.
She never got involved because as she always said
we would be friends again before the week is out
and we were. I never had long lasting scars and I
didn't hold grudges.

    We would spend time in each other's
bedrooms singing along to the radio or tapes into a
hairbrush, making up dances and charging people
to watch us lol. We would tape songs from the
radio, trying to cut out the talking, poised with one
finger on play and one on record waiting for the DJ
to shut up. Then once again the challenge to hit stop
before they started talking again. I remember one
time much later listening to the charts and someone
actually wrote in and asked the D.J. to leave a gap at
each end of a song so she could record the whole
thing hahaha. My tape collection from then is full of
blunt ending songs with random titles on the paper
insert. The funniest part though is the naming of the
songs, for years I thought the Carpenter's song "
Calling Occupants of interplanetary Craft " was

called "calling Arcupants", I honestly thought it was an alien name pmsl. I refuse to admit the age I was when I found out !

Some of my childhood friends are now friends on Facebook and it is nice to reminisce and share photos and memories.

I also had enemies too and it is amazing how years later when they attended A and E with their brats, they would assume we were besties at school and they assumed they could jump the queue. I guess everyone chooses their own version of memories.

Incidentally when we did have fall-outs, I only ever told mum what they said, I never told her I was just as bad.... that's the thing, kids do only give their version of events and My mum was smart enough to know that and never really took sides unless she knew all the facts.

Sometimes I wonder what parents are thinking when turning their children into victims by labelling others as Bullies. Don't get me wrong I don't condone bullying and I am not naive enough to think it doesn't happen but c'mon pick your fights. I was bullied, I learnt how to handle them and not become a victim. (Sometimes that involved my brother but hey ho)

Everyone has something that is different, children notice this and act on it. How the child reacts is what makes the difference. If someone said I had a peg leg I said " yes, I do and?" this works better than calling them to the headteacher and creating a scene, doing this can make the bullying backstreet, unseen footage that can't be proven but could cause a child to kill him/her self. Talk to your kids, hug them and help them to be strong whatever path you decide to go down.

I was once going to the St Johns Ambulance group at a local school and as I entered the school grounds the usual room was empty, I was looking around and saw a group of girls at the corner. One shouted over asking what I was looking at, I told her I was looking for the St Johns Ambulance lot and she came over, she started shoving me and saying I was staring at her, then the other girls came over and they started hitting me. As the group leader came around the corner the girls disappeared. He just said "Oh we are in a different room" and showed me where to go. He never even noticed what had been going on and I didn't know who the girls were so just went on as normal. Now these are what I term as Bullies but they never come to justice because they are sly. It's odd he didn't notice the state I was in though; did I always look this disheveled or was he afraid to ask ?

The zero tolerance only works if it is followed up and, in my experience, this is where schools fail.

A word of advice : if you know your difference, learn to love it and if someone insults you, thank them, this removes their enjoyment and can stop bullying in its tracks before it even gets to be a physical problem.

(*My daughter once called one of her brother's Asian friends fat and ugly, I was about to tell her off when he told her not to be racist .... woah WTF? She was being mean and name calling, this is not racism, she was six and he was twelve. I asked him to leave before I told her off.*)

I remember an old lady once getting mad at me, I was walking home from school with my brother and she started shouting at me " Stop taking the piss !". I had no clue what she was talking about so carried on walking. She lifted her walking stick and started to hobble after me, I started to run, the more I tried to get away the worse I walked and the angrier she became. Then I realised: "Oh, she thinks I am faking the limp". By this time my brother was howling laughing as he followed and she chased me almost all the way home, I kept shouting for Mick to tell her but he just followed us laughing. Thankfully she never caught me up but it was scary.

Real Bullies rarely stop when they leave school, they go on to be bullies in the workplace. I hate to see people being belittled or bullied and I will stick up for them. Sometimes sticking up for others can backfire, they usually back down and you are seen as the antagonist, but I won't stand by and be an observer if I think something is wrong regardless.

I hate this mamby pamby world we live in where everyone is afraid to say what they believe, afraid of hurting someone's feelings, having to be wary of 'isms' and being accused of racism, ageism, sexism etc. for saying what everyone else is thinking. I am convinced this is closely linked to the increase in mental health issues.

The new fashion of non genderising a child is beyond my comprehension too. If your boy wants to be a girl, then by all means go for it, let him wear a dress and call himself Mabel but save all the invasive surgery and medical intervention until he/she is competent enough to make an informed decision (Bear in Mind the legal age of consent is 16 for sex, and 18 to vote)

My daughter wanted to be a unicorn when she was six but there is no way in Hell, I would have considered a horn transplanted into her forehead. Incidentally, she wanted to be an orphan too so she could be like Tracey Beaker living in a Children's home, and that wasn't in my life plan either so she is stuck with me!

I have had three hip replacements now, the third was a revision, I don't have three legs in case you were confused. I now have knee problems and biding my time until they need replacing too. My son once told me I was probably worth more dead than alive with all that Titanium. I told him by all means weigh me in when I die, don't let the crematorium have it. I kept the implant from my revision , I was going to turn it into a paperweight. It looks like the inside of a hardboiled egg.

I have learnt to love myself, my faults and imperfections. I don't let them define me. I remember an online friend once saying that I didn't talk with a limp, that is so true !

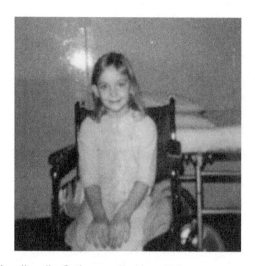

In Woodland's Orthopaedic Hospital

CHAPTER THREE: EDUCATION

My dad took me for my very first day   at school, Reevy Hill Infant School in Buttershaw, I was 5 years old. When we got there, he saw a little girl on her own crying, he said it would be nice if I could go look after her because she was sad, I sat next to her on a carpeted step and pretty much forgot it was my first day too as I comforted her. Maybe that is what geared me towards the caring profession, well that and or fact I told my Orthopaedic Surgeon once that I wanted to be a Ballerina or a nurse and he suggested nursing. He said it was probably the best move with legs like mine.

I loved it at infant school, I never felt sad going there, I was an eager reader and progressed through the ladybird books on a daily basis, I would read the Janet and John books in one sitting. The carpeted step of my first day I learnt was the reading step. Every day you would have a chance to sit with the teacher looking through a book and reading to each other, it was my favourite place.

We would go the church hall once a week to visit the mobile library and choose a story book, there were Great big wooden bookcases and the lady would open them up ,I was fascinated by all the colourful books. We all had a library card and I used to change my book sometimes when I went to Brownies, the mobile library was there after Brownies every week too.

There was no such thing as a snow day when I was at school. You went well wrapped up with two pairs of socks in your wellies and everyone changed in the cloakroom into black school pumps, if you were really posh you had white ones that were a little more expensive. There was always the box of lost pumps that you could use if yours were missing or you forgot them. I can still smell the dusty pumps ; some were that ragged with fronts hanging off and souls peeling off. I am more inclined to think they were ones discarded when replaced rather than just lost. The pumps were often used to discipline the naughty kids too. There was a similar box with clothing in, that box came in handy when I wet myself in assembly once.

When we moved up to the Junior school it wasn't quite the same, the class had two levels so I was in the same class as Michael. I felt like it wasn't 'my' place any more but more following in his footsteps. I was away from school with hospital appointments and surgeries that often I would miss out on the long-term friendship bonds that are made at the start of the year.

We would travel on a double decker bus each week to go swimming at Wibsey Baths, I often sat with the teacher on the bus as everyone was paired up. I guess I talked too much because one day she told me to do a sponsored silence and she would give me 10p when we got back if I kept my mouth shut!

There weren't fancy changing rooms with showers then, but rows of cubicles down each side of the pool with floppy curtains to maintain your dignity. Boys at one side and girls at the other. The swimming teacher was a real battle Axe. She told me I had the worst breast stroke she had ever seen as she poked me with her wooden stick, this was probably due to my hip but things like that were never considered and my teacher never corrected her. I still managed to get two certificates so I must have done something right.

We walked to school every day, sometimes I walked with my brother and other times with friends. There were lollipop ladies on every road so it was safe, I guess. One of the Lollipop ladies made me cry, she said " hurry up peg leg I haven't got all day !" I told mum when I got home and she phoned up to complain, I never saw her again.

I joined the school choir, the teacher was very fussy about who could join, there was none of this everyone can join in business, you had to audition, basically it consisted of reciting the scales forwards and backwards. I couldn't manage it in reverse the first time but I practiced and practiced so the second time I auditioned I got in.

The choir was really good and entered lots of competitions. We did a production of Sound of Music and Joseph and his Amazing Technicolored Dream Coat in collaboration with the neighbouring school. They did the acting and we did the singing. I got to sing the solo parts and I loved it. The only disappointment was mum never came to watch , I didn't have anyone in the audience to impress and at the end when all the parents came buzzing around their kids I just had to wait to be picked up and taken home.

I rehearsed for a school play one year for weeks only to find out I was going in Hospital and wouldn't actually be taking part, I was gutted. The teachers must have known and my understudy must have been elated.

When I got home from hospital, we got a VIP seat at the front to watch and mum and came with me , I remember thinking how it was strange she would go then but not when I was taking part , it saddened me a little.

I also joined the recorder group. One harvest festival I was playing recorder, singing in the choir and I had a little speech to make about thistles.

I had played the first tune and now sat at the choir bench, my recorder on the floor in front of my feet, I was introduced and stood with pride to walk over to the microphone, stepped on my recorder and flew across the stage at great speed landing splayed on the floor. I stood up like nothing happened and made my speech with tears in my eyes shaking from head to foot, I hate thistles, prickly little bleeders !

Nothing was banned from the playground, we had lots of fun at playtime, Wooden stilts that made you feel ten foot tall until you fell off, then out came the teachers with the wet paper towels and gentian violet, boy that stuff stung like a bitch !. Most kids had a purple splodge somewhere compliments of playtime , we had skipping ropes which could be used for skipping or reigns to play horse and carriage, there was no end to the use of a skipping rope, there were balls of every shape and size, I would play two ball against the wall with tennis balls. , you could play side by side with a friend and copy each other's tricks, or take over from each other mid trick, a lot of the ball games had songs too but I can't remember any of them, sad really these old games and traditions have been allowed to die.

Tiffany brought a note from school once offering skipping classes after school for £2, I told her I will teach her for free and her friends for a quid ! It is ridiculous how these simple little things can be commercialised. Even playing a recorder at school comes at a cost now !

You could of course play with anything you brought from home. I loved clackers, those little wooden balls on a string ,so soothing while they went right : click, click, click then BAM ! right on the boney bit of your wrist, I was black and blue from those things. Oh, and the elastics, they were fab, I have no idea where they came from but we all had them, super long strong elastic bands we would wrap around our ankles stretched around the legs of the two "enders" to form a rectangle while another child did tricks dancing inside the gaps. It was every bit as skilled as skipping was.

Playing British Bulldogs in the playing field , ramming into anyone and everyone to get through was a challenge but it was all part of growing up, no one was allowed to wrap themselves in cotton wool unless they wanted to be a loner.

When I moved to Upper school I hated it, Buttershaw comp was a whole new ball game. Before you even went you would hear the rumours, like all new kids would get thrown off the wall, in reality the wall was about 3 feet high and separated the top playground from the bottom with slopes down either side. but when you are only 11 years old it sounds like 20 feet in the stories, My Nan said if anyone threw me off, she would throw them off head first and I believed her ha-ha. The secret was to not stand in the top playground , simple.

I wasn't there long before we moved house, and I had to get a bus to school from being 12-year-old. The school special bus only took those with a free bus pass but we didn't qualify. A boy three doors down did because the distance was calculated "as the crow flies", and his house was outside the border whereas our house wasn't, what a stupid way of doing it ! The regular bus was always heaving and took ages to get there so I would get the earlier bus rather than be late, Michael usually got the bus at the last minute so we rarely travelled together

There was a bicycle shed at school, known as the smokers shed by virtually everyone, I never saw a bike in there in the whole 5 years I went there. Kids went in there for a crafty smoke or to sell their dinner tickets to buy cigs with. Those on benefits or low incomes would get their dinner tickets each day so would sell them cheap each day in the smokers shed. We didn't get free lunch tickets and mum would give me the money for the week on a Monday to buy five at a time. More often than not I would buy from the bike shed each day with my daily snack money and use the weeks money to buy cigs or sweets. The teachers would randomly check out the bike shed and anyone caught would get detentions , lines or sometimes caned if they persisted.

I was in there once and oddly enough I wasn't smoking at the time, someone said "here

,hold this a minute" and handed me a cigarette . I obliged and before I knew it found myself being dragged out by a teacher. She had seen him coming and offloaded her cig to me. I got a detention and 300 lines, "I must not smoke on school property" Denying it was futile, how do you say you weren't smoking when you were caught with it in your hand ?

They weren't as bad as the lines I got in cookery though. We made homemade lemonade and I was tasting it from the jug, the teacher saw me and gave me 200 lines " I must not drink out of a jug in cookery when there are perfectly good drinking glasses available" it went onto another line so you couldn't do it the fast way: writing each word in a column, it seemed so much faster as you didn't have to think of individual words. I got my own back though when she made us bake cakes for the school gala and half the class sprinkled salt on top instead of castor sugar. Someone even turned the teachers oven up to full too while she was distracted ha-ha.

I did enjoy cookery and learnt how to cook a lot of different things that I still cook today, my baking is strictly Bero cookbook though. I have tried so many others but always go back to Bero. Most of the things I made in cookery were eaten on the way home on the bus.

I chose needlework , cookery and art as my choice subjects for CSE's (*I was in the middle band so couldn't take O levels , although if you passed with a high mark, it was equivalent of grade C O level*) I hated academic stuff so thought I was being smart choosing the practical subjects, no one told me you had to learn a lot more than basic cooking and sewing, I had to plan menus, learn about food groups, different fabrics, and history etc. That is not what I signed up for !

In Upper school I was known as 'Mick's sister' virtually everywhere. For some it gave instant respect, but from the teachers I was branded a trouble maker and a class clown, although I don't ever remember doing anything to justify that judgement. It did save me from being thrown of the wall a few times though.

I also had some teachers who had been Joyce's teacher and expected better of me, she was the smart one and so I was given different treatment depending which member of the family had been in a class.

History and Geography were the worst, I was

encouraged to clean the store cupboard or given a chitty to go home for an hour and watch crown court rather than them risk me disrupting the class, as you can guess they had Mick in their class before I came along. I was a little annoyed because I learnt nothing in those classes and History was one of the required O levels to get into nursing school.

In PE / Games I struggled, I couldn't keep up and one time I was hit on the hip with a hockey stick accidentally. I could hardly walk and ended up having a week off school. Mum sent a note saying I should not be allowed to do contact sports. At first, I had to put on my kit and was made to sit the whole lesson watching everyone else, I resented them having all the fun, just sitting there   I got cold and uncomfortable and still hate watching any kind of sport, when I complained that I wasn't getting any exercise they let me go swimming instead.

One time someone had stolen sweets and money from someone else's bag in the changing room. When the teachers did a search of the changing room, she planted the things under my towel on the bench. I told the teachers what she had done but as I had been in there alone, they believed the girl over me and sent a letter to mum. I was no longer allowed to go swimming unsupervised. Mum was so angry and disappointed with me. I felt let down that no one believed me. This had a huge impact for when I did need to talk to someone and was convinced no one would believe me anyway.

We did cross country which I hated but as it wasn't contact sport, they made me take part even though I said I struggled to keep up. There was a specific course you had to take that basically went around the parameter of the Buttershaw estate. In the earlier years I could take a short cut down the snicket near home and go home for a break. I would rejoin the group as they crossed the field behind my house and cut out almost an hour. This changed when We moved house and I had to do the whole thing.

My form teacher accused me of talking once and when I said it was someone else, he came over and tried to move me away from the desk, he pushed me into the corner of another desk and my hip hurt so much, I fell onto the floor and couldn't walk. I was carried to the sick bay and given paracetamol and the pain wore off, I was so mad at him I pretended it still hurt and they had to get mum to pick me up. I was taken to the hospital and the doctor said I should have bedrest for a while until it settled. When we got home mum phoned to complain about my form teacher and it was the first and only time, I heard my mum swear on the phone, I must say I was impressed.

I managed to stay on the sofa for two weeks, laid with a blanket and left to fend for myself all day because mum had to go to work. I perfected emphasizing my limp every time I had to move when anyone was home. In the end I got bored being home alone every day so I went back to school.

The teacher was so apologetic and tended to leave me alone after that. I heard he had a reunion a few years ago but I hated him so had no desire to go thank you very much.

I had my first proper fight there. Some girl who kept hanging around me and my mates and I didn't want to be her friend, I told her to leave us alone and she went round the school telling everyone she was gonna kick my head in after school. As I walked out of the school gates she jumped me , we were surrounded, what seemed like hundreds of people shouting "fight, fight"

I had no choice but to fight back, after a lot of scratching, kicking and hair pulling she ran away. As everyone walked away, I saw one of my friends there, I told her my mum would kill me for fighting and asked if I could go to her house to clean up, I had a few bald patches and I was covered in blood, who's blood I have no idea. I ended up staying overnight at my friends to avoid any questions .

The next day I was called to the heads office.

I entered his office and I was terrified " I hear you have been fighting?"

" Yes sir" I said with my head bowed

" And who won ? " He asked

" I did sir !" I said with a smile on my face.

" You think it is funny ? "

" No Sir" then I looked up and looking through the window were some of my friends , I cracked out laughing, big mistake

I ended up getting caned for fighting, but extra ones for laughing. I had to stop myself from crying because I still had an audience but boy did it hurt !

When I got home My brother had told mum

and I get another smack for acting like a wild animal and sent to bed. I just thought there is No justice , after all she jumped me and I had no choice !

When I left school, I did not have the necessary qualifications to do my nurse training so I enrolled in the pre nursing course at Bradford college. On day one we were told that we were now adults and not at school. We were responsible for our own education and if we didn't attend, we would be thrown off the course and they didn't write to our parents. I respected that and it definitely encouraged me to attend.

I loved college, the tutors were great and the course focused on what I wanted to do, nursing, in the first year I completed all my necessary o levels .

In the second year the focus was on Anatomy and physiology for nurses, nursing terminology and nursing clinical skills, we even did a first aid course.

There were lots of gaps in the curriculum to take other subjects in that second year, college at that time was free so it made sense to fill the gaps with other subjects. I decided to enroll in Math's City and Guilds, social Studies and a Makeup and Photography course.

None of my new courses went down well and I ended up quitting after just a short time, the first was my fault. I was just not interested in the sociology class, the only thing I remember is people ate onion skins to get nutrients, the teacher was so boring I could not help myself from messing around, she threw me out the class one day and I never went back

The mathematics was ok, I enjoyed the work but it turned out we were entered into the wrong math's exam at the end, we still managed to pass with credit even though there was nothing we had learnt over the year.

The make-up and photography started great. We would get into pairs and do each other's make up, mostly theatrical : I had been made up as a skeleton and a doll, lots of photos were taken, we took our own cameras but the teacher took the films to develop. On the third week I was chosen for a complete makeover, a model for a day. We all went outside and walked around the streets and the park, I had lots of photographs taken, some posed, some candid. When we asked for the photos, the teacher said there was a delay in development but not to worry we would get them.

All seemed well until one day my friend did not turn up for the class, the teacher said he would be my partner, it seemed like a good idea but as he did my makeup he leaned in real close and said he wanted to kiss me. I shrugged it off thinking he was just playing with me. " Yeah right !"

After the class the teacher called me over, he said I could only have the photos from the photoshoot if I went personally to his office to collect them, I declined.

The walk home involved walking down a snicket, as I walked down there alone, he suddenly appeared in front of me and blocked my path " I told you I wanted to kiss you" he said grinning.

I was stunned and didn't know what to do, I got ready to turn around and then I saw my friend walking up towards us behind him, I shouted out to her and he just walked off. I told her what had happened and she said I should report him.

I told our course tutor the next day and he just brushed it off and said I should just ignore him he was probably just messing with me, it just seemed to be the story of my life. I quit the photography course after that, I didn't get any of the photos from any of the classes either. I had visions of them being pinned all over his office wall like you see on those stalker movies * shudder*

I spent a lot of my time at college playing pool as I didn't want to go home during free periods to be alone with my step father, I would hang around until I knew someone else would be at home.

Such a strange description for a abuser

My daughter is a groomer ...cutting dogs hair, washing and brushing them, making them look amazing with pretty little bows in their hair.

But this kind of groomer is a predator, preparing a child for their pleasure. They come from everywhere, often places of trust, they enter into people's homes and now they even seek prey on the internet.

I can't remember how old I was when mum met him, probably about eight or nine ,he was a Ukrainian man called George (well that was his English variant of his name). He once said jokingly that he only married my mum cos he wanted a little girl, he had a son from his first marriage and now he was too old to have children. Everyone thought he was great taking on another Woman's children. Only I knew what he really meant.

He would buy me things, clothes, a record player and records, he gave me money and took me on trips. To the outside world he was such a

63

...armer and he made mum really happy. They went on 'proper' holidays and Me and my brother even went with them to hotels at the seaside. He took mum abroad, as far as I know that was the first time too. She loved him so much and had total trust in him, after all he didn't *look* like a paedophile.

It started subtle, a kiss goodnight, he would come up to my room and say goodnight kissing me full on the lips, he always smelt of alcohol and sweat. He would touch my chest or leg and smile lecherously .It was around this time I started wetting the bed, a classic sign I learnt with my paediatric training. George would 'help' me take a bath when babysitting, showing me how important it was to rub the skin after I wet the bed to make sure all traces were gone and to get rid of any dead skin, who has dead skin under ten years old? I was too naive to even know what was happening at that time. I never mentioned it to mum as I thought this was what everyone did. I was so young when my dad died, I didn't really understand what a fathers role was.

George shared a house with some friends and sometimes when mum was working, he would offer to babysit, me and my brother would go over to his house. As George didn't work it was ideal to have a handy babysitter during school holidays. He would encourage me to sit on his knee while we watched TV and his hand would travel up my leg and up my skirt, looking back at some of the clothes I wore he didn't have to go far, my dresses were really short. He would stroke me through my pants and it felt nice so I didn't stop him, Like I said I was very naive. He would Call me his princess and buy pretty dresses for me, short of course.

I shared a room with my mum and when he stayed over, he would invite me to her bed after mum got up, he would stroke my hair, my arms, my legs and then inside my knickers, he asked me if it felt nice and I said yes so, he asked me to try and stroke him too, I suppose I gave my first-hand job under 10 years and had my first orgasm before I was 11. It is hard to think back now but at the time I was totally oblivious to sex and this just felt like someone being nice to me for a change.

We were once at the park and while we sat basking on the grass in the sun, he took off my knickers and sat me on his lap, he jogged me up and down gently with his fly down. He was singing some Ukrainian nursery type song and trying to teach me the words. No one could tell what was happening because my skirt was placed strategically over the naked flesh.

I remember years later after I was married, we went to visit and mum said George had made friends with the new neighbours and taken her two little girls to the park, I felt sick inside. I went next door and told her he was a pervert and she was probably best not letting her girls be on their own with him. I didn't go into details but she made excuses after that.

We went to his brother's house to visit but his brother wasn't there, he told me his brother had some antique dolls in his bedroom and showed them to me. He told me if I was good, he would give one to me. I was thrilled. We went into another room and he performed oral sex on me. It didn't hurt and felt nice so it never occurred to me that it wasn't normal. He never penetrated me, I doubt he was able to, to be honest looking back he wasn't that well equipped.

The sexual encounters became more frequent, every opportunity he had. I never thought anything about it until we had sex education at school. At that time sex education was taught around the time girls were expected to have periods, around 12 or 13 . It never occurred to me that this is what we were doing. I must have been so thick! This is when I tried to end it. He told me that they probably wouldn't believe me over an adult, he was well liked in his community and to many he was the perfect gentleman. He said if I told anyone they may take me away from mum or worse, she may hate me for it. I could make mum so unhappy if he had to go away so it was better just to keep it between ourselves. When I got more persistent, he put the guilt trip onto me saying I enjoyed it too and I never complained when he bought things for me. He told me I was no better than a whore and everyone would know that if I told them. He said he paid for what he got and I had no right to complain now. I just accepted it and believed what he said. I didn't want mum to be sad and I didn't want to be the one to break up the family if it was my own fault. After all no one believed me half the time anyway.

I rarely took friends home because I was afraid, they may suspect something and that would give people more ammunition against me, I blamed myself and I never thought for a minute that telling someone may actually make it stop. I even tried to poison him once, I put bleach in his sauerkraut, he didn't try it but after a while it went very pale and the cupboard smelt like a swimming pool so I threw it away.

Mum and George were getting married. At the run up to the wedding I told him we should stop because he should only be doing these things with mum and it felt wrong to go behind her back, I was around 13 or 14 years old. We moved house and I had an attic bedroom of my own next to my brothers. I started to avoid him but he would make excuses to come to my room. He started to hurt me if I complained, subtle and not leaving any marks. Even when people were around, he would try touching me, If I said anything, he would call me a liar and tell me to get over myself. By then I was developing breasts and he took every opportunity to stroke one or grab my bum as I passed him, always making sure no one could see. It would have been obvious to everyone by now that things were different but I think I was just seen as a rebellious teenager being mean to her step-father.

Because I had put an end to the encounters, he started to become nasty, he called me a prostitute and said he paid for what he got. He made me feel cheap and dirty. He did stop coming to my room at night because I would shout 'GET OUT' at the top of my voice if he tried and by then my brothers were in the room next door. In public he was the perfect step Dad and no one suspected anything (well as far as I knew , nothing was ever said , no questions were ever asked)

It was only a problem when we were home alone, he would make a pass at me and he would hit me, by now I was seen as the antagonist so he didn't care if he made a mark. I stayed away as much as I could when mum was at work. I stayed at Dennis and Angela's house a lot and became close friends with Angela. She was a great support, I told her about the physical, and emotional abuse but never told anyone about the sexual abuse because I still felt ashamed of it and that I had brought that on myself and at that time he wasn't hurting me.

At 16 he insisted I went on the pill. He said if I didn't, I wasn't allowed to go anywhere with my friends, he said did not want me bring a 'Bastard' back to 'his' house. He persuaded mum to take me to the doctor to get a prescription. No one asked any questions; I had an examination but as I was still technically a virgin nothing was said and they gave me the pill. I was convinced he wanted me on the pill for himself but there was no way I would be leaving myself in a position for that to happen.

At 18 I started my nursing career. I lived at home because at that time I was still wetting the bed and too embarrassed to tell anyone about it. He wasn't working and spent every day sitting at home playing cards and drinking. I was at home studying and he tried again to make a pass at me, by then he was like Rab C Nesbit. Sat at home all day in a string vest and dirty long johns with his privates showing. I pushed him away and he went crazy, he picked up his walking stick and started to hit me with it. The bruises were deep and rose into big lumps on my arms, legs and back. I ran from the house and phoned mum at work. She said ' I must have asked for it '. The problem was he was careful to hide his actions but made sure he got a good reaction in front of people so that I looked like the antagonist.

I went to stay at my brothers for a while because I was angry with mum and scared to go home. With hindsight I should have gone to the police but at that time I was still convinced no one would believe me.

I was very close to My Cousin Julie, I used to

stay at her house at the weekends, I came so close to telling her what was happening but got scared in the end, his words ringing in my ear how it was my fault, I had encouraged him and was quite happy to receive gifts and money so anyone would see I was just a prostitute. I didn't think she would believe me even though she did know he had been hitting me. I became depressed at times because I was at constant war with myself and I guess my cousin got sick of my miserable face hanging around. When she began dating again, I saw less and less of her. Looking back, I know she would have believed me, I should have trusted her but that is easy to say years later when you realise you were not the only one this had happened to and the brainwashing is so deep set you believe everything they say.

I really thought I was giving these signals to men; was there some kind of subliminal message I was giving off that only perverts and paedophiles could, see ? Why would anyone believe me ?

I never understood how so many people knew about the physical abuse yet no one ever did anything about it. I guess it was a different time and if my own mum thought I asked for it what chance would I have with a stranger. I never told my siblings, although one time when he hit mum in a drunken rage, I called David and all my brothers came round to give him a warning, then would have been the perfect opportunity, but it was about mum being protected and I didn't feel I should add to the problem.

When I did return home, I made sure I was never home alone with him again. I didn't talk to him at all and I studied in the library. When I wasn't on shift, I left home at the same time as mum every day. Eventually he gave up.

When parents complain about children having sex education at primary school, saying they are too young. You are never too young to learn what appropriate and inappropriate behaviour is. I just think how things would have been different if I had just a little bit of education before it started, just enough to tell me something wasn't right, an opportunity to say something at the start.

I found out later that George had been accused of abusing his son in his previous marriage and that is why he was divorced, such a shame that men can move on to another relationship and repeat this kind of behaviour whilst looking like the perfect gent to the outside world.

I remember being at My cousin Sue's in Blackpool, I had gone for the weekend with Julie and her kids. there were family members there, Aunties and Uncles. They were talking about George and how nice he was and how he made my mum happy. I wanted to scream and tell them what he was really like but instead I just sat there quiet seething inside. That night I wet the bed; I was devastated. Julie told me not to worry and said she would tell everyone it was her daughter, but I know Sue knew, I was so ashamed but angry that he could still have that power over me even away from home. I stayed upstairs for a long time just feeling stupid and disgusted with myself. What could I say ? Even when Julie came up to sort out the bed, I felt embarrassed but she reassured me and persuaded me to go down. I just acted like I had a hangover so as not to make anyone suspicious.

George developed a brain tumour and didn't last long after that, I liked to think it was justice before he got his dirty hands on any grandchildren. I guess if he hadn't died, I would have to tell everyone for the sake of the next generation.

CHAPTER FIVE: THE CHURCH AND ME

I was not baptised as a baby, Mum felt everyone should choose their own religion when they are ready. I didn't know this until I was about 12

I went to Brownies and Girl Guides as a child. I think most people did then, there wasn't really much else to do when it was cold out to be honest.

Once a month the Brownies carried the flag in the church, I think it was a kind of agreement as the brownie group was held in the church hall. On nicer days we would have a parade through the estate and that was fun too, with the marching band of the boy's brigade and local scouts and guides.

Anyway, one Sunday when in the church I was approached by a member of the church choir and asked if I would like to join. She was impressed with my singing and thought I would be an asset; I was already in the school choir so this sounded like fun. I always enjoyed singing

The church was the one place I felt safe, it seemed soothing even on bad days when I entered the church. Joining the choir was the next step up, I guess.

I really enjoyed it, the singing, the 'uniform' and especially when I earned my Surplus and gold medal. We even got to sing at weddings and for that we got paid, real bonus !

The problem with the church choir like everything else is they had the good and the bad and me being me seemed drawn to the bad, it was there I started smoking, in the toilets of the church hall. Always seemed ironic to me that mum trusted these people more than the rough kids from the estate yet my bad habits were learnt in the church choir . Another thing that bugs me with judgmental people, I guess.

After a year or so I was asked by the vicar if I wanted to join the holy communion class so I could take communion in church and have my first holy communion when the bishop came for a special ceremony. I was attending church every week , twice most Sundays so I was really keen.

I attended classes for a course and on completion was told he would need my baptism certificate to complete the paperwork. "No problem" I said not realizing I had never been baptised. I was devastated when I found out. The whole class that attended with me were about to take their holy communion and I couldn't.

The Vicar said I could do it the following year instead but would need to be baptised first. My mum then informed everyone so the whole lot of us got baptised together, I was almost 13 then and the older ones were obviously adults so it seemed a bit weird to me.

At 13 I was then able to take my first holy communion in the Church of England. Mum bought me an amazing dress and shoes, pure white and I felt like a bride. I was so excited.

George said I had to wear gloves but there had been no mention of that in the preparation , he bought some cream gloves at the last minute. They clashed so bad with my dress and I didn't want to wear them. He said if I didn't wear them then I couldn't go so in the end I agreed.

When sitting in the church none of the other girls had gloves, they laughed at my ugly cream ones and said I should take them off. I asked the Vicar and he said I didn't need them so I took them off. After the ceremony there was a party in the church hall, but My step father went berserk, he dragged me from the church all the way home, he said I didn't deserve to go to the reception and I had no photos taken in the dress either. Mum later gave it to one of my cousins to play dress up in, I was gutted.

I was fascinated by the Organ and when a music teacher from school started playing in church, he offered to give me classes for 50p a week. I asked mum and she agreed. I only went once as I realised, he wanted to teach more than the Organ. He gave me the creeps and I couldn't get out of there fast enough. I daren't tell mum so I just didn't go again and spent the money each week. After a few weeks I told mum I couldn't manage the pedals and had quit, she seemed to accept that

It didn't stop me going to church I just made sure I was never alone with the organist. I quit the choir when I started college as I had a lot more study to do and could not commit to regular choir practice. I continued to attended church frequently until I started nursing and that made it awkward with shifts etc. Sometimes I went to a different church with my cousin and her family if I was there at the weekends.

I had always dreamed of a big church wedding but when I tried to Marry my first husband in Church the vicar refused as they said he had been married before even though it was a registry office so I ended up getting married at the registry office. I still had the white dress and bridesmaids so I didn't feel too disappointed.

The church offered to bless the marriage but that didn't make sense to me, why would the church give a blessing for something they refused to do ? It still doesn't make sense to me. I declined because to be honest I found it quite hypocritical.

After I had Daniel, I wanted to get him baptised at the local church, they refused saying we both had to attend every week before they would consider it. I worked shifts and My Ex refused to go on his own. We went to another church and they said they would do it as long as We got permission from our local Church as he didn't want to tread on anyone's toes. We managed to get permission and so it was all arranged.

Daniel was baptised and we put his name down for the school connected to the church. Not long after that we moved house. When it came time for Daniel to go to school/ Nursery they refused saying we no longer lived in the area. The school local to us had a pretty bad reputation so we appealed the church school's decision. I was accused of being racist because I wanted him to go to a Christian school so my appeal was denied. By now I had totally given up on My Church, they were never there when I needed them yet I had dedicated a lot of time and energy to them.

I considered home schooling at first or private school but by then we had Nathan too and I knew we couldn't afford private tuition for two children. At this time mum attended the Catholic Church, she had converted to Catholic when she married George as he was Ukrainian Catholic. I had been going to the Catholic Church with mum most Sundays and although I was not allowed to take communion I felt accepted in the parish.

Mum suggested asking for Daniel to go to the Catholic school so I made an appointment with the Priest, he asked why I wanted a Catholic school, I told him I didn't , I wanted a Christian school and this was the only one in the area. He thanked me for my honesty and told me they have to take a percentage of non-Catholics and he would prefer to fill a space with a Christian child. The school board agreed to accept Daniel and from then on, I never went back to the Church of England. Nathan and

Tiffany were both baptised as Catholics and all three took their holy communion in a Catholic church, not bad now considering I have an atheist, a white witch and a fence sitter lol.

I took my first holy communion as a Catholic at the Easter Vigil before Tiffany took hers in the June the same year. The hardest part was the confession, I was terrified. I had to make an appointment to chat to the priest beforehand as there were a few things I had done that I later regretted.

I told the priest that I knew My step father had no sense of smell and I thought the best way to kill him was to poison his food, I told him what I done when I was twelve. I had to be sure it wasn't something anyone else would eat so decided to put bleach in his Sauerkraut because it stinks anyway so less detectable. People started commenting on the smell of bleach in the cupboard and I just said I had been cleaning it. In the end I ended up throwing it away. So where do you start with this in confession ?

I told him I hated my stepfather for what he did to me and I couldn't see a way to forgive him. It didn't really have an impact because he was dead by then anyway.

The priest just sat and listened, he asked if I was sorry for what I had done and I said obviously at the time I wanted him to die to put an end to my suffering but with hindsight I did think it was a bad idea and I did throw the Sauerkraut away so no actual harm had happened to him. The priest said the decision was made as a child and as a child my thoughts would be different, he said I should just forget about it and move on. So, my first confession was "I swear a lot and shout at my kids". Not much has changed really. At my last confession when I said I swear a lot the priest asked if it was in anger, I said "no , I just open my mouth and it comes out" I could say I tried not to swear, but I would be lying.

My attendance in church has been sporadic over the years but my faith is still strong, I never felt more at ease or safe that I did in a Church. I still hate confession but at least it has gone from needing a 30-minute appointment to a quick , I swear a lot Kinda thing.

The way confession is taken has changed a lot too, it tends to be more of a counselling session than a trip to the headmaster's office. The penalties are more or less the same, a few Hail Mary's and Our

Fathers with an addition that I actually enjoyed. I was asked to think of 5 things I was thankful for and spend a few minutes with each one and appreciating it. A good exercise for anyone , especially if you are feeling a bit down.

Many people are shocked to hear I am religious because I swear a lot and don't give the goody two shoes impression. I feel religion is a private thing, I think everyone has a right to believe or not, everyone has a right to be of whatever religion they want. It is not for us to judge nor force our beliefs or none beliefs on others. I have lived , I have had a lot of life experiences that make me look and act like I do but inside I am a very caring person and once you really get to know me you would not doubt my faith.

Chapter Six: The First Marriage

I met My first Husband, in the September of 1985 at the nursing home, he was the handyman and was sleeping in a room in the nursing home 'for convenience' although I later learnt it was because he had nowhere to go after splitting from his wife 2 years previously. He had a mattress on the floor and the place looked like a tip.

He was a charmer, he complimented me and flirted with me all the time at work but I think he did the same with a lot of the girls. .

I was going on a work Christmas night out and informed Angela it was about time I lost my virginity so "tonight was the night", she laughed and told me to have a good time.

I had a great time and he sat and chatted to me most of the night, I actually fancied his friend but he told me he was married so pointless going there, at the end of the night he offered to take me home in a taxi, when we got to the house, I felt I would be ok he would have a coffee and leave and anyway Angela would be back soon. I went to the toilet and when I got back there was a note in His hand "I think this is for you" he said laughing

GONE AWAY FOR WEEKEND
DON'T DO ANYTHING YOU WILL REGRET IN
THE MORNING
LOVE ANGELA x

Shit!

So, he stayed the night and I did lose my virginity, he was gentle and understanding and it felt right. In the morning we shared a taxi to work but he was careful to come in after me so no one would suspect anything. We continued to see each other out of work   and after only two weeks he said he loved me and would wed me, I just said "yeah right" and thought nothing of it.

Then I realised I was late, as in two weeks late, the one time I have sex and I'm late! I took a test the same day I realised and it was positive. After a minor panic I phoned him and told him I was as much to blame as him so I would understand if he didn't want to stick around. I told him I don't believe in abortion so I was gonna be keeping it whatever he decided. He was ecstatic, he said he loved me and knew from the start he wanted to be with me. He proposed to me there and then, the ring came a few days later.

It was such a short time but I honestly believed I loved him too but I think now I loved the idea of being in love, all my friends were marrying and having babies, I was 24 and only just lost my virginity! (Seems ironic I had been on the pill since being 16 years old until I left home and never had reason to be)

When we told everyone, they were shocked at how fast it happened, my mum tried to warn me not to rush into things but was there to support me in my decisions. My cousins Kath and Dennis at the pub offered to let us use the room for free to have an engagement party and Sue offered to do the catering. We had an engagement party between Christmas and new year.

We got a turkey as a Christmas gift from the nursing home, everyone got one but the manager said as seen as we were together, we could have one to share. My fiancé was so mad , he said if we are sharing, we are getting the biggest one. When he got it home it was too big for the fridge or the oven lol. Sue said to take it around to her in laws as they had a big oven, she said we could cook it and use it on the party buffet. I went round later that day to bring it home but he said it was at Sues and she had left us the legs, they were HUGE ! I walked round home chewing on mine like Henry the eighth lol.

My fiancé bought me a puppy as a gift, a Yorkie, he was gorgeous, I named him Frederick Von Dinkybum, or Dinky for short. I had so many people coming up to me saying "A dog isn't just for Christmas" I understand their concern but sometimes they have to realise that dogs born near Christmas need homes too and I had no intention of getting rid of him! I had Dinky until he was almost 16.

My fiancé told me his mum had not been as accepting of me at first and told him he could do better than a cripple! why would someone tell you that? Should have been a red flag there for sure !He could have kept it to himself. She was usually nice to my face but after what he said I never really liked her. I called her the dragon after that, but not to her face

In February I started bleeding and was put on strict bedrest, but despite that on valentine's day I miscarried, I was devastated! My fiancé came to visit me in Hospital and informed me he had booked the wedding for June because he didn't want me to think he was only marrying me for the baby, I thought it was such a nice gesture but with hindsight it was probably the start of him taking control.

We were messing around at his mums shortly after that and he gave me a horse bite on my leg, it really hurt and I told him to stoppit, he told me not to be such a baby and did it harder. I walked out and went home. Several hours later he came home drunk and began shouting at me, I was laid asleep in bed so it all seemed to happen so fast, he punched me in the eye and gave me a cut and black eye. Afterwards he apologized and said it was an accident he meant to hit the headboard but his watch caught me, I half believed him because it happened so fast, I could have made a mistake in how it happened. I was shocked by his rage over nothing but he said he had too much to drink and it built up, he apologised profusely.

I was Godmother to Michael's daughter Rebecca that Sunday and my brother was furious, the photos were not good with me in sunglasses. He got together with my other brothers they cornered My fiancé in the club toilets and gave him a warning that this better not happen again. They tried to warn me he wasn't a good person but I just made excuses for him, I stuck with the story that it was an accident.

About 3 weeks before the wedding he came home drunk and was verbally abusive, he demanded I get him some food and I told him to get it himself, he grabbed hold of my hair and banged it against the wooden chair arm repeatedly. I went upstairs to get dressed and said I was leaving until he calmed down, he went berserk, he threw the TV off its stand across the room and threw the ironing board through the glass bedroom window. By then a lot of neighbours had gathered and were shouting up for him to stop and the police were called. he stormed out of the house.

I was a wreck when the police came. The police arranged for the window to be boarded up until I could get it fixed and advised me to go somewhere else for the night in case he came back. They never asked if I wanted to press charges, I guess it would be more paperwork for them. I don't think I would have but it may have made me realise how serious it was. I picked up Dinky and went around to Sue's house as I was afraid to stay at home and I didn't want to go to mum's for her to say I told you so...

I went home the next day to sort out the damage and just hoped he wouldn't come back.

Over the next week several of his relatives came around pleading on his behalf saying he was broken inside and regretted what he had done. They said he was drunk and didn't know what he was doing and it was so unlike him. I stupidly gave him a second chance. I think with the wedding planned I was too ashamed to admit what had happened to anybody and this seemed the best option. I begged Sue not to tell anyone and agreed to speak with him. My fiancé was so apologetic and promised he would never do anything to hurt me, he said he was angry about something else and because he was drunk, he didn't realise what he was doing, he said it would never happen again.

We couldn't get married in church as he had been married before so I compromised and had a white wedding with bridesmaids at the register office. I was disappointed but the day was really nice and we had a reception at the Ukrainian club catered by some of Georges friends. My new husband was on his best behaviour.

We had a Honeymoon in Paignton compliments of his mum, it wasn't really what I wanted but it was a gift so I just went along with it, we didn't have much spending money because My husband was owed some wages and the guy said he could not pay him. There was supposed to be entertainment in the hotel but it was geared towards the elderly and boring for us, with what little money we had he bought a fishing rod at the gift store and spent most of the week fishing. I just sat on a bench to read my book. I was due on later that week and once again I was late, I took a test when I got home and it was positive.

A few weeks after we got back from honeymoon there was a knock on the door in the early hours of the morning. The police came in and arrested him, he told me not to worry it Was a misunderstanding and he would soon be home, but he wasn't home until later the next day. My husband had been charged with Arson and endangering lives. He told me that on the night before the wedding he had gone around to his old boss's house and asked for his wages, he had been promised it for the honeymoon. He was told they did not have it so he had taken the fuel pipe off his boss's motorbike and set light to it, the bike had exploded and taken away the end of the house with it. I had seen the article in the news but never thought for a second, he was capable of doing something like this.

Apparently, the guy he was with at the time had seen the news and decided to go to the police before he could be identified as being near the scene at the time and told them what happened. I thought it was strange that his boss didn't turn up for the wedding as he was supposed to be his best man, my husband just said they had a disagreement about the money so he told him not to come, his step dad ended up being best man.

He appeared in court a few months after and was sentenced to 18months in prison. I was gutted, I was four months pregnant and alone, no job, no income and had barely got the things I needed for the baby. It was all over the papers too so everyone knew about it and it was awkward to say the least. I felt like I was the one being punished not him.

I applied for benefits but were told that the only money I could get was unemployment benefit which did not even cover the mortgage. Then I went to a pop-up benefits workshop and they told me everything I was entitled to which was more than double. Apparently benefit offices only give you information on what you know about and don't tell you about extras you are entitled to. This is something worth knowing if you are in financial need, take advice from other agencies and don't rely on the government offices to tell you what you are entitled to.

I visited him a couple of times in prison but he sent most of his visitor passes to his step dad and he was only allowed visitors once a month. We wrote almost every day and he would say how sorry he was for the way he behaved and how everything would be different when he got home with the baby.

I had hoped they would give him leave to come for the birth but they refused so my mum was there with me when Dan was born. When I went into labour the plan was to take my dog to mum's house in a taxi and pick her up and then she came with me. Her house was close to St Luke's so that seemed ideal. Except the taxi took ages to come and I was stood outside in the middle of the night biting holes out of the door casing waiting for it. My neighbour came over to see if I was alright and stayed with me until the taxi arrived. She was so caring; she had her coat over her nightie and it made me laugh seeing her cross the road. Nowadays neighbours are more likely to be watching you through the window and videoing a show for YouTube!

After my son was born, I had good support from family and friends, I had word that My husband had put in for parole so with one third off for good behaviour he would be home in around 6 weeks if it went well. I took Daniel to see him in prison but it was horrible, they even checked in his nappy to be sure I wasn't sneaking anything in. There were no changing facilities and I had to feed and change him on my knee in the toilet, it was definitely not a place to take a newborn.

My mum had put a birth announcement in the paper, stating it was our first born, apparently his first wife contacted him to say it wasn't his first and sent him a picture of his son who was around 3 or 4 at the time. He looked a lot like the boys in my family, blonde hair blue eyes, I still don't know what that was about, she left, ran away to Scotland and refused any contact, yet she had his details in prison and wrote to him ?

When he came home, and for a few months after everything was perfect, we didn't really go out to the pub and we didn't have much money for alcohol in the early days so it wasn't a problem. He was very insecure and would assume every time I left the house; I was seeing someone else. He said Daniel looked like my nephew and accused me of having an affair with my brother-in-law, I reminded him my brother looked like him too and even his son from his first marriage looked the same but he still gave me 'that look' that made my hair stand on end.

He hated if I went to visit friends or go out with them, he would say "if we have money to go out, we should go out together we never go anywhere nowadays" it was subtle so I never suspected he was just trying to keep me to himself. He was rude to many of my friends so they stopped visiting and so he became very important to me too. As long as I towed the line and stayed by his side everything was perfect.

When we did go out that is when the fighting would start, well I say fighting it was him having a go at me with some bogus accusation, "I saw you looking at the guy behind the bar" "who was that guy you said hi to?" and when I tried to explain he would explode, he rarely hit me but he would throw things at me and around the house, break things I liked, and push me around. It was more about control, letting me know who was in charge. This wasn't enough to leave him for, was it? He would always apologize and things would be great for a while.

One night I had been to visit a sick friend, I was taken to her house by another friend and as we chatted it got late, it was around 10pm when I got home. My husband went crazy, he was drunk and asked where I had been, he said "look at the fucking time" and threw a clock at me. I tried to explain I was relying on a lift so couldn't just come home but he got madder. I told him if he carried on like this he would have to go. He went upstairs and got Daniel out of bed, he said If he was going, he was taking his son because he was not losing another son. He could hardly walk and was holding Daniel like a rag doll. I persuaded him to sit down and said all I wanted was for him to calm down and that I had no intention of throwing him out it was a spur of the moment thing. I managed to get Daniel off him and back into bed as he fell into a drunken sleep on the sofa. The next day he apologized and so the cycle continued.

I felt as though it was my fault, he made me

feel like it was my fault every time and so I was ashamed of myself for letting it happen. I didn't tell anyone because I was too embarrassed to admit it. I changed my behaviour to stop it happening.

These episodes became less and less as I learnt how to keep him happy. I refused invitations and made excuses for anything other than work or family parties where he came too, but even that did not keep him happy, often we would get home and the alcohol fueled fights would start again. He did realise that if he drank lager, he was fine but if he drank cider, it made him aggressive. Most of the time I persuaded him to have lager.

I had problems with the local Childminder after I had Nathan so when he was about a year old My mum moved in with us to help with child care, I didn't have any concerns about that because by then all was calm in the house. It worked well for us both, mum had company and the kids had a continuity of care when My husband worked away during the week.

The original idea was for us to move and go to a seaside town, somewhere better to bring up a family

As a father he did very little with the children and we relied a lot on mum even when he was at home. One night I was cooking tea and Nathan was being particularly whingy. My husband asked me to sort him out because he was watching TV, but I said I was cooking so he asked mum to, Mum said she had had him all day and why couldn't he look after him.   they got in a bit of a debate and in the end, I brought him in the kitchen with me. I had him strapped in his pram and he seemed content getting the attention. My husband came into the kitchen in a rage and started throwing things in his usual Paddy. Mum came in to try settle things down and he attacked her threatening to hit her if she didn't back off. This time he went berserk, he even threw a wall unit over before storming out of the house. Mum said she couldn't stay with us after that and moved out. Once again, he returned with his tail between his legs and apologized.

I was stuck for child care again then; at the time I was working in Accident and Emergency and luckily work agreed to change my shifts. I started working four until midnight on a Friday and a late shift Saturday and Sunday. This meant my husband was home at the weekend and so he was responsible for them. This did not last long though he said "I don't work away all week to look after Your kids at the weekend" Oh ok, MY Kids?

We had a babysitter who agreed to look after the boys at the weekend but only if she could take them to her house because she said   my husband creeped her out when she was on her own there. Red flag right there I missed ! Things were calmer at home for a few years. Then my husband had developed an ulcer; he was rushed into hospital after a massive bleed and the doctor told him if he carried on drinking, he would be dead in 6 months. He stopped drinking for about 6 years.

When Tiffany was born everything was great for a while, my husband seemed to be his old self, he was on beta blockers for high blood pressure which the doctor said could have been a reason for his bouts of rage. Unfortunately, he didn't like how they made him feel so didn't take them for long, he still didn't drink so as long as I didn't do anything to antagonize him things went pretty smooth. I never let my guard down though.

The babysitter looked after Tiffany from about six weeks but she was starting college, I went back to the old child minder and she agreed to have

Tiffany one day a week and the boys after school. The babysitter would pick them up from her house when she finished college. One day she came back and found Tiffany alone in the kitchen, she had just her nappy on and was sobbing, I was told she looked like she had been sobbing for ages. She shouted for the child minder but she didn't answer . The child minders husband was in the living room, he said she had gone for a shower and Tiffany hated him so he just left her in there. The babysitter picked her up and she never went back.

I changed my shifts so I only worked a late on a Friday, Saturday and Sunday, that way the babysitter could have them as before.

When Tiffany was about two, her dad had heart surgery, he was off work for a while. This seemed to have a sobering effect on him too. Things were great for the next few years.

I had my hip replacement when she was just 3 years old, she was at nursery but I had to keep her at home because nursery wasn't considered compulsory and I struggled to get her there

This was the second time I fell on a recorder, about two weeks after my hip replacement I stepped on one at the top of the stairs after my bath and went down every step on my arse leaving the towel on the top step. Tiffany was so young at the time and incapable of calling anyone for help. I had visions of ambulancemen I knew coming to get me, trying to work out how to get some clothes on when I couldn't move, should I call my sister to get me dressed first? in the end I just waited for the pain to subside enough until I could stand up, it was a week Later I told my husband and suggested I get it checked out when I seemed to be limping a bit more than usual.

We moved house when Tiffany was about 6. The new house was lovely, in a nice neighbourhood and backing onto woodland which gave the kids somewhere to go play and let off steam. The Babysitter didn't like travelling to the new house so in the end I agreed to let Daniel look after the other two at the weekends, he was 14 at the time. Daniel was brilliant. Not only did he care for the kids he kept the house tidy and usually had a hot drink waiting for me when I got home. Unfortunately, this changed when his dad came home and he had to be a kid again. He was always mean to Daniel but he just shrugged it off

My husband's brother was home from the Army and they spent a lot of time together, he started to drink again and so began the paranoia and abuse. He would shout at Daniel for no reason and intimidate him. The boys tried hard to please him but all the time he just put them down, it must have made him feel in control. He had learnt that his words didn't bother me any more I had become complacent but if he was to have a go at Daniel, I would defend him and that is where he got his power back. He even accused me of having an affair with Daniel's best friend one night just because he saw us laughing at something, he didn't feel was that funny. They were 16 years old at the time!

We did have some good times as a family but most of the time a great day was ended with him having a drink and undoing all the good stuff. He would also expect me to pay for everything, even asking for petrol money.

We didn't really have proper holidays; we would go camping or just have days out. and when he got a payout for a work injury, he promised the kids we would go to Disneyland Paris, we got all the brochures and information and even sent for the video showing what the park looked like and the kids were so excited. I applied for us all to get a passport because my husband's had expired and none of us had ever been abroad.

The week after he got the money in his bank he went on a shopping spree, he bought a new fishing rod and he started going to the auctions and buying ' antiques' that he felt was an investment, he was hooked, he even bought a box of plastic costume Jewellery for Tiffany because he knew she liked pretty things. It was junk !

The money went down and when I asked about the Disneyland holiday, he denied ever saying that, he said it was his money to spend how he wanted and another row started. I didn't want the kids to be totally disappointed so I told them the money wasn't quite enough but we would still go to France and booked to go to a Eurocamp. As usual I ended up paying for it.

When we got there it all seemed idyllic, there was an outdoor pool and lots of activities for the kids. All he wanted to do was hang around the tent, drink beer and have a barbecue in the evening. We had a few days out but to places like war memorials and he seemed to be following his grandads footsteps from the war. I tried to get him to take us to Disneyland for the day but he said he didn't come all that way for that.

The kids were bored. Daniel even started marking the days like he was in prison, he wasn't allowed to do his own thing even though he was 14, he was expected to play with his brother and sister. I took them to the pool most days but when we got back to the tent, we were facing the Spanish inquisition, where have you been, why were you so long, the food is ruined and so it went on , more drink, more aggression.

When the sun went down in the evenings it got really cold. I was sat in the tent kitchen inside my sleeping bag still feeling cold. My husband brought the BBQ inside. It just had the red embers and gave off a little heat. Shortly after I was woken by Tiffany crying. Her dad yelled what was wrong and she said she needed a drink, he yelled for her to get one then. As she made her way to the kitchen I could feel the walls of the tent swaying, like she was leaning on them, she said she felt dizzy so I got up to help her. She was shaking and pale, I figured she had spent a lot of time in the sun and was maybe dehydrated so I knelt on the kitchen floor and laid her on my knee, I offered her the drink. She said she felt sick so we went outside, as I stood up the world began to spin. My husband got up and after a few expletives went over to the toilet block. As he left, I tried to call out but no words came out I fell to the floor, I was aware of myself fitting and wetting myself but unable to move or control it, Tiffany started to scream. I told him what happened and he told me it was just some kind of hysteria and to shut up because I was scaring Tiffany

When they went back to bed I wondered if maybe the BBQ was giving off fumes so I brough it back out, by now there were no embers just ash.

I started to vomit over and over; my head felt like it was going to explode. I shouted for help and in the end a doctor was called, When the doctor arrived, he feared I may have carbon monoxide poisoning and wanted to take me straight to hospital. My husband followed in his car after telling Daniel to keep an eye on the other two.

When I got there, I was almost unconscious, I had bloods taken which showed such high levels of carbon monoxide they needed to refer me to the hyperbaric centre miles away. They told My husband he would need to have bloods taken too and also the children; they would not allow him to drive. The doctor told me if Tiff had not woken, I would have been dead in the morning.

The hospital sent the police to the camp site to collect the children, poor things must have been terrified. After blood tests Tiff and her dad were sent back to the camp and Daniel and Nathan were kept in hospital overnight on oxygen. In the meantime, I went in an emergency ambulance to the hyperbaric centre.

I was placed in the hyperbaric chamber and had a mask strapped to my face, a young medical student was sent in with me to explain what was happening the first time but after that I was on my own, My French was poor, junior school poor, and I had left the phrase book in the tent. There was no offer of an interpreter. !!

I had to have a course of three treatments and each time I could feel my head clearing, it was like the best hangover cure ever ! I was in a two bedded ward and the old lady in the room with me understood no English, every time I wanted something I would ask her what it was and then ask the nurses, the nurses were horrible, all they would say is 'no English' and walk off, If I had said ' no

Urdu' to a patient in Bradford I would have been sacked!

There was an en-suite toilet in the room, I had been given a gown but still had the same dirty knickers on that got wet when I had a fit 2 days ago., I wasn't offered anything to wash with and I couldn't ask for it, I used the other ladies toothpaste using my finger as a brush and her soap to have a wash, using paper towels. I rinsed my knickers out and placed them on the radiator, I felt dirty and disgusted with myself.

When I was transferred back, I was sent in a taxi, there was a meter in the taxi counting Euros up at great speed, I had no idea how I was to pay for it because nobody explained. I had no money with me either. The journey was over 3 hours, funny it seemed like 10 minutes when I went there. When we arrived back at the A and E , thankfully there was no mention of the fare, I had more bloods taken and discharged, The Campsite had upgraded us to a caravan for that night. The first thing I did was have a hot shower and put fresh clothes on.

The next day we travelled home. I needed a holiday after that !

***

As Nathan got older his behaviour became more erratic, he was in trouble at school and constantly testing me, he would lie and steal. I once said if he wasn't my son, I wouldn't let him in the house. When his dad was home, he became a recluse and spent a lot of time in his room or stay out of the way. I thought he had ADHD but it became apparent later he has a form of Asperger's. I was advised by the Chemist to give him starflower oil which helped his concentration and his school reports improved greatly. It was suggested he go for an assessment but His dad stated "No kid of his was going to a shrink!"

As My husband worked away and I was tied to the house on an evening , that is when I started to chat to people online. I met some amazing friends online and felt able to tell them my problems and got support without being judged. I found it hard to sleep at night and there was always someone to talk to online 24 hours a day. Nigel was a good friend, my soulmate, we chatted for hours, we even talked online when my husband was at home but as we were only friends it didn't pose much of a problem. My husband once asked me if I was having an affair and at the time, he asked I can honestly say I wasn't.

I used to confide in My friend Jane and we often chatted online putting the world to rights. My husband even accused me of having a Lesbian affair with her because I would put xx after I said bye. Jane had witnessed several of his outbursts and asked me what it would take for me to leave him. She told me one day he would kill me and his behaviour was getting more erratic every day. I tried to stick up for him by saying Alcoholism is a disease and I wouldn't leave him if he was a diabetic. She sent me a link to show me what she meant. It basically said if someone knows they are aggressive after drinking certain alcohol and not with others then if they drink it, they are choosing to be aggressive…this was my wake-up call! He knew if he drank cider or wine, it made him aggressive but he chose to drink that over beer which had little or no effect.

I decided in June 2004 to start preparing to leave. I opened another bank account and put any spare cash in there. I got all my paperwork in order, passports, bank books, birth/ marriage certificates etc. and kept them together in a wallet for easy access.

I had started to see Nigel occasionally and we became very close. I wouldn't have left My husband for him and he knew that but he still lived with his wife so I guess we were equal.

When Daniel was 17, he had been late home one night and his dad locked him out, told him to sleep in the dog kennel if he was cold, it was bouncing with rain and cold, Dan sent me a message " I am staying at my mates, if he lets me in or not tomorrow, I don't care but don't worry about me " The next day after another bout of verbal abuse by his dad Daniel told me he was leaving home. I was devastated but understood why. He said he couldn't live with his dad any longer. I knew just how he felt !

Daniel moved to Hull to live with his Girlfriend. We drove Daniel there and his dad refused to get out of the car, he told Daniel he would never be welcome back if it didn't work out. That was the last time Daniel ever spoke to him

After Daniel left things got worse, he turned his anger to Nathan but Nathan wasn't as placid as Daniel and argued back. I tried to defend him but it just backfired. One night after a particularly hard shift I returned home to find my husband drunk (nothing new) He was sat in front of the TV with beer in hand and the kids were upstairs creating havoc. The kitchen was a bomb site and the living room like tin can Alley. As I walked in at 9 pm he asked me what I was making for tea. Quite often I would go without rather than start cooking when I got home but, on this night, he was insistent there was nothing to eat. He had given the kids a combo of freezer food and said there was nothing else. I said there was meat and fish etc. in the freezer and fresh veg I thought he might have made a dinner, but he meant no 'instant' food i.e., sausage, chicken nuggets, oven chips or burgers, something he could make without effort or chuck on the BBQ. He would fill a tray with different junk food and throw it in the oven, as he always did a combo there was nothing there, he hadn't already had recently.

I went into the kitchen while he was still shouting to find something and he followed me in, he opened the deep freeze and one by one took everything out and threw it at me. He said I was lazy and the house was filthy. He said he didn't know why I had a cooker because I never cooked anything for him and that it was probably filthy behind it, he then proceeded to pull the cooker away from the wall and it was clean because I had done it during the week. This angered him more so he ragged it out and tried to throw it, he bent the door he dragged it that hard. He picked up the dirty dishes he had left and threw them at me. By now I was cowering against the door. The place was trashed. He then told me to clean it up and left me there. The back-door key was not in the lock and I didn't have my phone with me. I was too afraid to get up and go out of the kitchen so just started cleaning everything.

At 4 am I went up to bed. I just laid there afraid to sleep. My husband got up and left for work at 5:30. I made the decision then to leave him there and then. It was two weeks before Christmas, the savings I had weren't as much as I had hoped but was enough to buy some essentials while we sorted ourselves out. I had all the important paperwork, and bank books etc. all together

I didn't want to go to mum's or family as I didn't want him to go causing trouble on their doorstep so I called my friend Angela to ask if we could go there today so I had some space to sort out somewhere to go and she said I could stay as long as I needed but she was leaving for work soon. I got up and packed the bare essentials in a rucksack. Put the kids Christmas presents in a bin bag and rang a taxi. I woke the kids and without telling them where we were going, I put them in the taxi and we left.

CHAPTER SEVEN: NURSING CAREER

I always wanted to be a nurse, especially when ballet was ruled out due to my crap balance and inability to dance.

I joined the St Johns Ambulance when I was a teenager and enjoyed learning new skills, I especially loved the attendances at galas and fetes, sat in a caravan or portacabin administering first aid to those in need. I felt like a VIP in my grey uniform dress and white paper hat, almost like a proper nurse .

I started working voluntary at St Luke's Hospital when I was 15.We had moved to a house just a few streets away. I just walked into the first building which happened to be the hospital kitchen and asked where I should go if I wanted to work voluntary, they directed me to the admin building where I met Mrs. Hogarth the nursing officer. After a little chat she took me along to the acute medical ward C3 and introduced me to the ward sister.

Sister Busfield was a very 'old school' sister and was pretty regimental in her ways, she was a firm believer in everything looking clean and tidy. The bed wheels had to face the same direction and all pillows should have the opening facing away from the door to keep the draft out. She would do a walk down the ward inspecting all the beds and patients to make sure it looked perfect before letting in visitors. I would watch her in Awe, the level of respect she demanded was so high you could almost see her glide down the ward.

My first tasks were helping the ward orderly, giving out drinks and helping feed those who couldn't feed themselves. There were porcelain spouted mugs which were pretty easy to use once you got the hang of them but I was afraid it would pour down the patients necks so went extra easy at first and placed a cloth napkin under their chin. One lady had a ginormous glob of phlegm around her mouth so she couldn't open it, I called over to the nurse to ask what I should do, "just wipe it off" she said, I almost threw up. I am still not a fan of mucous or phlegm, I would help set out the trays and tables for mealtimes, laying a placemat down with cutlery and a napkin along with a mini salt and pepper, it was so fancy compared to the picnic type trays they send for patients now.

Sister Busfield loved to give out the lunches and would roll up her sleeves placing white cuffs on to keep her uniform smart. She always went around asking if they had "quite sufficient" before taking the trolley away. At breakfast time she would take any leftover sausages and place them in the warming cupboard for the nurses (a sackable offence now, they have to be thrown away, such a waste !). I would then go around and help Feed the patients. They also boiled the eggs in a huge pan on the stove top, any left over and the ward orderly would mix them with salad cream and place in the fridge for afternoon tea. I remember once she blended the meat from dinner with melted butter to make 'potted dog' for the sandwiches, there was very little waste then. I was sent to the kitchen to get the "Asian meal" at teatime, it usually consisted of a tin of Heinz curried beans that they would give in place of the meat of the day. A far cry from the Halal options offered nowadays.

After breakfast the orderly would boil the milk for the sisters and doctors morning coffee and hob nobs. Only the senior staff were invited to that. The other nurses would then have a quick cuppa and maybe a sausage or two before starting the daily chores.

As I got to know the ward better, I was able

to help the nurses, making beds and even assisting with bed baths. I even assisted on the back round where everyone's bum and back were checked several times a day, bedding straightened or changed and patients made to look comfortable. Work was allocated in tasks in those days so after handover the nurses would each be given a task; the bath book was kept up to date ensuring everyone had a regular bath or bed bath. The ward was in two halves, a male end and a female end. I always worked down the female end at first. One day I was asked to help a nurse with baths and she started walking down the male end, I tried to keep my embarrassment in and didn't want to refuse so just followed her. I soon got used to it and the men washed their own 'bits' anyway.

I was asked to help move a lady into a side room from the main ward, I was casually walking along pushing the bed and said " she doesn't look very well, does she ?' to which the nurse replied " I should think not she's been dead for two hours", I let go of the bed like I had been electrocuted, the nurse just smiled and said " its ok she won't bite" and so that was my first official encounter with a dead body at just 15 years old. I still don't like been left alone with one even now! (I heard of a man sitting up in the viewing room of A and E once after he died, I never trusted a dead body after that.)

Later that day I was asked to take the patients notes to the mortuary. I was terrified, I expected Lurch to answer the door so braced myself

A little guy with a squeaky voice opened the door, I was even more scared as it wasn't what I expected, I threw the notes at him and ran lol. He must have thought I was crazy.

I loved working on the ward and went every spare day I had, I felt appreciated and also found a great escape from home, at the same time I figured it would be welcomed experience when applying for my nurse training. The nurses on the ward were so encouraging, many advised me to go for Registered nurse training rather than Enrolled nursing as the job prospects were better.

At 16 I started college on the pre nursing course. I loved college. The topics were relevant and interesting, I had to continue with English and math's but they were requirements to access the nurse training. Although they did have a GNC test, like a Mensa test you could take if you did not have all the required GCE's. I failed my English exam in both years, well I got a C which wasn't high enough. This amused George who said all those foreign students could pass it but I couldn't and I was English, he did not understand it was a different exam for foreign students.

The Nurse recruitment officer came to college to talk to us, I asked if I failed my English would I be able to take the GNC test and she said "what makes you think if you fail English, you would pass the GNC test?". OUCH! I felt about two inch tall and everyone was laughing. She also asked for a letter from my consultant to say I was fit to nurse. I wrote to Mr. Wishart's secretary for a letter and he replied with "If they cannot tell if you are fit to train, they should improve the medical assessment and not bother consultants who discharged someone years ago " Classic response, I couldn't have put it better myself ha-ha

I had continued to work on the ward while at college, every weekend and Wednesday afternoons. Even when I had a hospital placement, I was placed on my usual ward which was great. I took the GNC test and got 98%, I was turned down by the Bradford school of nursing (I think she remembered me and wasn't impressed by the consultant letter). George stated that was because I was still working for free so they didn't want to pay me, maybe he was right who knows. It did seem unfair considering Sister Busfield gave me a glowing reference and I had shown my dedication over more than 3 years.

Luckily, I was offered a place at Airedale and Calderdale but the acceptance letter from Airedale was stand offish and made it sound like they were doing me a favour, but the director of nursing in Halifax sent a lovely letter welcoming me to the school of nursing, so I decided to accept Calderdale

My First day of nursing

I started my nurse training at the Willows, Calderdale school of nursing, in January 1981. The school was based in a detached house across the road from the hospital. The Royal Halifax Infirmary (*Named wrong apparently by the Duke of York at the opening ceremony, it should have been the Halifax Royal Infirmary*) It had a nice homely feeling to it, not like the universities of today that are so regimental and still feel like school.

My first day I miscalculated the bus times and arrived late. My journey was 1 ½ hours with bus changes and the timing of connections, so if one missed or was late it would make a huge difference to my travelling time.(*I know mum told me she lived near school and if she was late, she was late, the teacher had said how come someone from far away can get there on time, Mum told her it was easier to catch up if you lived far away*), I suppose I could have got a Taxi to make up the time but I didn't have that much money.

I apologized for being late explaining how far I had travelled and was met with "Oh you can't be from Bradford you are the wrong colour". Not the best of starts and not sure it would go down so well nowadays. We were all kitted out in our uniforms at the start of the day, we got a new one each week for 6 weeks and they were then ours to use for the whole three years. A blue and white chequered dress, no sign of trousers on nurses then except on the men (and the very rare Muslim nurse). We were given a beautiful blue wool cape, lined with red and a red strap that crossed over at the front, just like you see in old movies. I wish I had kept it; I think I left it hanging at the back of a door in A and E and it disappeared. We were shown how to fold our hats and insert little studs in the back to keep them together. The hats were precut in white card, they were flat and they had different stripes for different levels, as a first-year student it had one blue stripe. You were supposed to fold it at the midline to make a neat hat but many with two and three stripes would fold them lower so the hat was higher and stood to attention. As a new starter we wouldn't have dared lol.

My first day got worse, I had been sat in the classroom all morning and then we went over to the main hospital for lunch. I donned my blue cape and walked proudly across the road, as I stood in the queue at the canteen a nurse approached me and said I look like I may have started my period, I thought I was just sweating with having tights on in a hot classroom but a huge red stain was over the back of my dress and no one had thought to tell me...thanks ! The nurse showed me to the changing room and showed me how to get a spare uniform from the auto valet, she gave me some paper knickers and a couple of sanitary towels. my own dress was thrown in a linen skip and I was told it would be ready for me the next day, I never saw the nurse again but she was a lifesaver!

After that failed start, things just got better, I loved my time in Nursing school although I didn't really socialise with anyone as most of the girls lived in and it was quite a commute from Bradford. There were a few cliques in the group but that never bothered me as I had never been one of the popular girls anyway.

I did watch a series on TV once a few years ago , I think it was called 1950's nursing, they took modern day nursing students and put them into the old style of training , it made me laugh because so much of it was like the 1980's when I trained, so little had changed by then.

My first ward was a male Orthopaedic ward, we would have fun and the banter kept us going

"Nurse, can I have a bottle please ? "Nah you will have to wet the bed" all the time knowing you were going to get the bottle, nowadays everyone takes things so literal you are afraid to make a joke for fear of disciplinary action.

One night on the gynae ward we were told the younger girls in the four bedded bay had gone to bed early and didn't want disturbing for their 10pm meds. The night before they had been up half the night talking so we decided to play a trick

We went in at 9pm and turned the light on, "Good morning, ladies", The look on their faces as they thought they had slept all night and still felt rough, we all thought it was funny , even the girls, how I miss the fun side of nursing.

As a Third year you would sometimes be expected to take charge, with only Enrolled nurses, auxiliaries or junior students on the ward with you. Nurses were prepared for taking charge and had the necessary skills. As a third year you were senior to an enrolled nurse which was stupid really as Sometimes the Enrolled nurses were so skilled, they would have been way better at it, some of them had been nurses longer than I had been born !

Nurses were expected to be the face of the health service at all times, you could travel in your uniform but you had to wear a navy gaberdine coat and hat when outside. I was in the community with the health visitor and my hat kept blowing off, she told me to leave it in her car. Later that day I had to go into the school to pick something up and the nursing director saw me

" Where is your hat nurse ?"

" I left it in the health visitors car by accident as it kept blowing off, sorry "

" Never mind I have one you can borrow" she said as she steered me towards her office. After a few minutes of rummaging around in a drawer, she brought out all I can describe as an antique hat, it was Navy blue felt but had patches of purple where the fabric had bleached over the years. She handed me the hat and a handful of pins "you can bring it back when you get yours back, don't let me see you without it again" I tried real hard not to look horrified

As I stood at the bus stop waiting to go home, with this multicoloured antique on my head I was conscious of the laughter coming from other nurses as they walked past. I never forgot my hat again that's for sure !

Another day she walked into the class as cool as a cucumber   " I have just been in town and seen two nurses eating pasties" followed by a large pause and 'Paddington like' stare around the room "out of a paper bag", she added with another hard look around

"You know who you are !" she said looking

over her spectacles and then walked out with a disgusted look on her face, oh she did make us laugh.

There was an incident where we had to meet in a foyer and there were limited chairs. We all raced to get a chair like we were having a game of musical chairs and one girl, Sue, ran smack into the side of my head, her nose exploded, I felt terrible but she never really blamed me and we became pretty good friends after that, she lived away from the college too so we would go to the bus station together and then go our separate ways, we would bounce terminology off each other on the bus and it helped a lot to have a friend. I visited her when she went to have her nose fixed, mostly out of guilt.

I did make friends with an Enrolled nurse Suzanne in my second year, she lived in Halifax and I stayed at her house a few times so I could go on a night out, she is really the only one I ever stayed in touch with. One of the patients had a huge crush on her but it was against policy to date patients, he kept asking for her number but she wouldn't give it to him. When he was discharged from the hospital, I gave him her number and said "she isn't your nurse any more so I guess it is ok "

They got together and got married. Suzanne had twin boys around the time I had Nathan, we kept in touch for a few years but like all friendships you drift apart as life moves on.

I found it hard to study and commute with all that was going on at home and failed my first intermediate exam, I was devastated. After that I went to the library every day I was off work and spent the day studying. I would tell My step father I was working as he was not very supportive of my studies. I tried to study at home once and he threw my books and told me to "get off my lazy arse and clean the house" this was all the while he was sat with a glass of whiskey, in his dirty undies and string vest playing patience with a pack of grubby playing cards.

I studied hard but it was tiring, working and studying and travelling. I found it hard to relax at home because I was made to feel guilty all the time and always looking over my shoulder for what he would shout at me for next. I wasn't sleeping very well. It was cold in the attic and the roof had a leak; it was dripping down from the skylight window onto my bed. I had a plastic tablecloth on top of my bed to stop my bedding getting wet but the constant tapping of raindrops kept me awake. George refused to look at it and said it was condensation and there was nothing he could do about it.

I went downstairs one night and sat in front of the fire to keep warm. George came down and turned off the fire and light and told me to stop wasting the power and go back to bed. I sat there in the dark and cried, I wanted my dad and I knew if he was still alive this creep would never have wormed his way into our family. I did get a Dorma built eventually and the 'condensation' immediately stopped.

Looking back this was a depressing time of my life. The one thing I wanted was to be a nurse and I was failing. Mum and George had gone away on holiday and I was alone for a week. I was struggling on my own and waiting for my results, I knew if I failed again, I would be off the course. I had no idea what I would do if I couldn't be a nurse.

On the Friday of that week, I decided that was the end for me and gathered every drug in the house and alcohol. I sat looking at all the pills, some mine, some mums, some George's, everything from strong pain killers to heart tablets. I played "Red Red wine" by UB40 over and over and cried to myself. I started drinking but then thought about how Mum would feel if she came home and found me dead, I thought "what if I fail?". A nurse who can't even take an overdose successfully...that really is a failure! Then the phone rang and it was Sylvia, my friend asking if I wanted to go out so I gathered up all the pills put them back where I got them from and got ready to go out. Sylvia saved my life that night and she never knew.

I told Sylvia I was feeling down and her answer was a weekend bender. I had never been on one of those before or since. We went in the kind of clubs that needed a special knock to get in, all night bars and night clubs, we came home about 7 am, a few hours' sleep and back to the local at lunchtime. Funnily enough I never got a hangover despite being permanently drunk from Friday evening until Sunday! The pubs were not open 24 hours like now and so we went home to nap before going back out on the night. It was a nice day so I slept on the sunbed but that was a big mistake I was so dehydrated and sunburnt; it is a wonder I didn't die of alcohol poisoning. I was drinking twice as fast when we returned to the pub that night!

The results of the exam came in and

thankfully I passed my resit so was allowed to continue with my training. I did really well in my practical work but always struggled with the academics (I still do!)

At the end of my training, I passed my hospital exam but failed my final exam twice. I was advised to take the Enrolled nurse exam instead because I was advised if you fail 3 times you have to retrain and cannot do that for 5 years. as the Enrolled nurse exam was multi choice and it was the essays I struggled with, this seemed the best option. I always knew the answers but never seemed to get the chronological order right. It is so much easier now with cut and paste . we hand wrote everything so difficult to add something once you have missed it. I passed the enrolled nurse exam but did not want to stay in Halifax, at that time a 3rd year student was senior to an enrolled nurse and it just didn't feel right taking a step down, especially after all the other girls passing first time and already working on the wards. The travelling was becoming a bind too, after three years of travelling 1 ½ hours each way it gets pretty draining.

I worked behind the bar at My cousin's pub for a while and applied for jobs but most of the jobs had been taken by those who passed earlier or who were from Bradford. I didn't really see myself as a barmaid after all that training so after a minor disagreement I walked out.

I phoned Susan my other cousin in Blackpool the next day and had a bit of a rant, she suggested I go over for a holiday and take a break from it all so the next morning I got on the coach. It was Friday and as Susan went about her business, I took a walk to the local job centre. I picked up a card advertising a job in a nursing home and took it to the counter, after a short phone call I was asked to go there the same afternoon. If only job seeking was like that now, it was so much easier with visible cards and dealing with a human rather than a computer.

I went for an interview for a night shift job, Monday to Wednesday one week and Monday to Thursday the next, alternating. The Job sounded great and the interview seemed to go pretty well.

Dennis and Angela came for the weekend and offered me a lift home on Sunday and as I had not heard back from my interview by Sunday morning, I decided to give them a call. "Oh, didn't they call you, I'm so sorry you start tomorrow " I was a bit shocked , I didn't even have any spare knickers, never mind work shoes and tights! Angela said they would be going home but she lent me her credit card to buy whatever I needed, she said I could pay her back when I got paid. It's a good thing shops are open in seaside towns on a Sunday and I managed to get everything I needed.

Sue and Howard, her husband, said I could keep my room for a minimal charge for board until I found something else. The world was looking bright again, new job, relocation and no George, the great escape had begun!

I loved working there, walking on the prom to work, sitting on the beach reading my book when the weather was nice and having Sue for company. I did get homesick sometimes as me and mum were always so close, I phoned mum nearly every day and visited at least once a month.

The local shop had a book exchange programme, you buy a book and when you finish you take it back as long as it is in new condition, you could exchange it for another book or get half your money back. I think I went through most of the books he had while I lived there.

The nursing home was great, there were 50

beds but most of the patients were pretty mobile. (Yes, patients not bloody clients !). I worked with just one auxiliary, I did the meds and she put them to bed , we joined forces for the larger patients or those less able.

The first lady I worked with Was such a lovely lady, the day staff had warned me she was a witch and a lot of people didn't like working with her cos she scared them, oh, OK,

The first shift we were just sat and she asked me who Leonard was. "What?"

"Yeah Leonard, he found out you were gonna be working here and he hasn't left me alone since, he said he was your dad" I froze my dad was called Leonard but last I heard he died when I was 6 years old, how could she know? I never met her before in my life and as far as I was aware she didn't know any of my family.

"Yes, that was my dad's name but he died when I was six"

"Yes, I know he is dead but he has been stalking me, he is pretty arrogant and said he won't go away unless I tell you he is looking out for you and is always there, oh and there is a dog sat by your feet too called Mitzi"

Mitzi was our family dog but she got run over when I was still a kid. So yep, I met the witch.

I asked Judy if she could see dead people like that why was she working in a nursing home instead of making money on the prom or like the clairvoyants on TV.

She told me it was a God given gift and if she used it for gain, she would lose it

"Never believe those commercial clairvoyants, they are blagging it because if you pay them, they see nothing!" She said "beware of open lines like "I see a man, recently deceased, name begins with a D, Dave maybe?""

Then the old lady says "My husband Dan just passed "

"YES!!! That's it, Dan, he wants you to know he loves you very much, blah blah blah"

I have no choice but to believe her because she was so accurate. I even told mum and she said "yep that sounds like your dad". So now when anyone goes to see these people I wonder if they are just scammers playing on people's emotions but I know they will still go so it is up to them, I won't be wasting my money.

Work at the nursing home was good, we enjoyed each other's company and once the patients were settled, we could watch a bit of TV or just chat, there were a few cleaning jobs and vegetable prep for the auxiliary to do but we just mucked in together. We had to walk around once every hour to do a head count and make sure everyone was ok, only on one occasion did a lady go out of the fire escape but the alarm went off so it didn't take long to find her

Sue's next-door neighbour was in the process of renovating some flats and offered me first dibs when they were ready so I knew I would soon have my own place. I am pretty sure during the summer months Sue and Howard were taking a loss renting the room out to me when they could have got a lot more from a holiday maker. I am also confident they wouldn't have thrown me out, but at the end of the day it was a business.

Howard had been Ill for some time and seen several doctors, he was more or less accused of being a malingerer by his GP and his health just went downhill. He lost loads of weight and I was really worried about him, and so was Susan. I told Judy and she said to bring something of his into work, something he used. I took in a handkerchief, and Judy held it in her hands, when she gave it back, I dropped it because it was so hot, she said it would give him a few days relief but she could only see Blue in his future , she said that meant he would be at peace.

Not long after that Judy left and I had a new colleague, Elizabeth AKA Betty, although it sounds older, she was only young but preferred Betty to Liz

She was funny and beautiful inside and out. She would ring the local radio station during the night and chat on there for ages, she made me laugh because she always had a valid opinion on everything and the chat show host loved her. We spent most of our time together, we worked 3 or 4 nights each week and the other nights we went out on the town and the days we spent shopping or going to the beach.

I was genuinely happy even though I did still get a little homesick at times. I missed my mum but knew going back to live with them was not ever going to happen.

Then the bomb hit us, Howard was diagnosed with cancer and given only months to live, I loved Howard, he was like the dad I should have had. Apparently, the reason why none of his fit garage mates asked me out is because he threatened them , I thought I must have been ugly, cheers Howard !

Sue had to sell up the business and move back to Bradford so they could both be near their families and also spend quality time together without worrying about work. I only had my work friends and I was offered a flat but I didn't feel I could stay there with no family or friends outside work so decided to move back to Bradford myself.

I told Betty and she was devastated, she begged me to stay but I could not see me being there away from all my family. We arranged to keep in touch and she had an open invitation to visit me anytime. The last message I got from her was just a few months after I left, she was supposed to come see me but had been so depressed and wasn't coping, she had split from her boyfriend and moved back with her parents.

There was no way I was moving back in with Mum and George when I returned to Bradford and by then Dennis and Angela had split up so she offered me a room in her house.

I got a job in a Nursing home as soon as I got back to Bradford so things settled down pretty quickly. Angela and I were a good team, we cooked for each other, shared the housework and got along really well. When Angela and Kevin decided to move in together, they wanted to move out of the house she had shared with Dennis so after viewing a few flea pits for rent I decided to apply for a mortgage and bought the house myself.

I couldn't get a 100% mortgage and although I had enough for the deposit it cut into the savings, I had for furniture etc. Angela said not to worry about it and she would give it back. So, I wrote a cheque for the deposit and handed it to my Solicitor, he gave it to Angela's solicitor, who then gave it to Angela and she gave it back to me. I was so grateful and it meant I was in a good position to set up home for myself.

After I met my First husband things got difficult at work, the manager was not happy we were in a relationship. Some of the girls told me she had the hots for him and that is why she was annoyed with us. I had the miscarriage on Valentine's Day. That was the day he booked the wedding for June the same year. After we married, she was even worse to me, expecting me to work with reduced staff and changing my shifts all the time. Insisting I work through my lunchbreak etc. When I became pregnant with Daniel, she made things as difficult as possible. She even insisted I lift a 23 stone woman with a 16-year-old carer with no experience, when I refused, she got real angry accusing me of being lazy. I ended up telling her where to stick her job and walked out.

One day My ex had to go into the nursing home to do a job on a Sunday, we were on our way out so were together in the car. When he went inside everyone was asking about me, A few of the ladies had asked me to visit so he came out to get me. I only stated for a short time but on the Monday morning the manager called me. " I hear you came to visit yesterday " " yes" I said, "some of the Ladies wanted to see me". " Well, you are not welcome on the premises and if you come again, I will call the police"

I was really shocked and when my Ex came home, I told him what had happened, I guess there were a few hormones thrown in because I was crying unconsolably. He was fuming and called her, he told her if I wasn't welcome neither was, he and he quit

Well, that was smart, A mortgage and a baby on the way and both of us unemployed. He told me not to worry as he could just work for himself and there was always work for people with building and electrical skills.

I never did go back to work full time after that but worked bank shifts in the library to keep the funds going. After I had Daniel ,his dad felt it was better for me to stay at home as he was earning enough self-employed to pay the bills. I used this time to resit my exams as time was running out and I really wanted to open my career to better jobs.

I passed my finals and was now a registered nurse, unemployed but registered . Seems ironic that after 2 years of working as an enrolled nurse just sitting an exam made me so much more qualified lol.

When Dan was about 3, I got a job in a private slimming clinic 2 days a week as a registered nurse, basically taking observations, weighing people and dishing out slimming pills.

The manager from the nursing home came in one day, she was all smiles, "fancy seeing you here" she said, " yes you are on my territory now though" I replied. When I weighed the clients, I would write it on a card and hand it to them, it was an unwritten rule not to call it out as they could be upset. When I weighed her, I took great Joy in calling it out. She never came again, strange.

I was called into the boss's office after about 6 months to discuss my wages, I thought I was getting a pay rise but she actually wanted me to cut my hours or take a pay cut. The cutting of the hours was basically a longer lunch break unpaid where the staff could come pull me out when someone needed pills. I decided to start leaving the building for my breaks rather than work unpaid for two hours each shift. I went to the park one day, The sun was blazing and I was enjoying my lunch when a police officer came over to me and asked what I thought I was doing... "erm having my lunch, in a park, on a sunny day ??"

Apparently wearing a nurse's uniform in a park in the middle of Manningham could be misinterpreted, so I was kindly advised not to make a habit of it WTAF ???

My sister worked in Manningham Library and it was maybe a ten-minute walk away, I did work bank shifts there sometimes so knew all the staff, they were happy for me to take my lunch there and hang out in the staff room a couple of hours on the days I was working.

The manager of the clinic realised I was not there to work for free and after discussing things with her financial adviser she said maybe she had made a mistake and that a pay cut would have been a better idea. She stated that she could get an enrolled nurse for less money and would not be offended if I looked for a different job. I started to wonder if it was true and I was getting paid too much, after all I hadn't been a registered nurse before and I hadn't worked for a few years. I decided to go check out other jobs in the job centre. Wow The pay was a lot more than I had been getting so I decided to move on, I initially started working on the nurse bank so I could get back into the true clinical setting I had been away from for about 4 years.

I found out later she tried to get an enrolled nurse but the slimming pills were controlled drugs so she needed a registered nurse, she tried to persuade me to come back but I declined.

It was around that time mum moved in with us , my ex was working away a lot with work and it was a perfect solution for child care.

I worked on mainly paediatric wards, ENT and general surgery. I got a few shifts on the Orthopaedic ward which I really liked and one day I was asked to help in Accident and Emergency.

When I got there, I explained it was a lot of years since I had been in an acute setting so they figured I would be best helping in the minor / suture theatre.

I was taken into the theatre and a nurse was cleaning a man's facial wounds, removing grit from his face with a scrubbing brush, apparently, he fell off his bike using his face as a brake. I was there about a minute and suddenly felt all peculiar, I asked for directions to the toilet and sat there the colour of wax with my head between my knees hyperventilating. I thought I was gonna pass out or throw up. After what seemed an age, I started to feel better, I washed my face and returned to the theatre, The nurse was almost laughing when she asked if I was OK, she wasn't daft lol.

The gentleman had gone by then and I just said it wasn't the blood it was a bit of a shock her using a scrubbing brush on his face like that, she explained she had numbed it first and all of a sudden, the world was ok again. I stayed in there, cutting the knots for the sutures and applying dressings, I had an amazing shift.

Shortly after that the bank bosses decided each of the bank nurses should have a designated area, at the time I was torn between Paediatric or Orthopaedic and trauma.

Around Christmastime the children's ward were having a Children's Christmas party with Santa and the works, the staff were told they could go home and fetch their children. I was asked to work later than my 1pm finish to accommodate this and help set up the party. I asked if I could bring my son and was told no it was permanent staff only. I said sorry but I had no child care after one so she would have to make other arrangements. It made my decision easier on which department to choose.

The sister on the paediatric ward was livid when I chose orthopedic and trauma , she tried to say I had a duty to them but I reminded her I was bank and not actually a permeant member of staff.

I was offered a permanent job in A and E and worked there for 11 years on a basic D band, each time I tried for promotion I was told only if I went full time. I had a young family and was not prepared to leave them 40 hours a week.

During my annual review I asked the senior sister if I could do my paediatric conversion and was told no there were no places, I felt deflated, If I ever went for another job how could I explain why I was on a basic band D after 11 years ?!

One of the other sisters approached me and told me it was not true and that two places were allocated to A and E each year but were rarely filled, she told me who to contact so that is what I did, I was told I was guaranteed a place , I just needed my managers signature on the form, oh and she advised me to do the facilitating learning course first to get me back into studying, by now nursing was university led and not nursing school so things were so much different.

The next day I went to see the manager, he asked if they knew I wanted to do it 'downstairs' I said yes, I didn't tell him they said no , and so the form was signed. The facilitating learning course commenced within a few months , it was one day a week in university and the rest was based in A and E. He began with " There is no such thing as a bad student, only a bad teacher "

The practical side was no problem, completing competencies was a doddle, but the written part, the assignments were a whole new ball game. I felt like I was cheating, so much is based upon quoting from books and very little brainwork. When it came time for the final assignment, I wrote my draft and handed it in, the tutor said it was

"Brilliant " "exactly what I wanted" and so I typed out the whole thing and handed it in, I was so confident and pleased with what I had achieved.

I Failed ! what ? how ? I had an appointment to discuss the assignment and to get feedback. I said "what happened to Brilliant and exactly what you wanted ?" Apparently, I had not done any Harvard referencing, "what ? what the hell is Harvard referencing ?"

"It is plastered all over the library I thought you knew "

"They advertise soap on the side of the bus but they don't sell it, why would I assume that was something I needed to know if my tutor did not tell me ?"

Anyway, I looked it up, added it to the end of the identical essay inserting names and dates and passed this time, the same words, the same work, the same format with added historical names in alphabetical order and bingo !

Kinda makes his first statement right, huh ? I have a quote; I hope I reference it correctly

" The facilitating learning course is a crock of shite" Carol B. 1999

The paediatric nursing course was basically open learning, it was for 18 months you got a list of assignments, a list of necessary hours and an outline of the course. I was still based in A and E but they had to give me time off half a day each week for study, a study day once a month in university and time off for placements once arranged.

I was responsible for arranging my own placements. I spent hours on the phone ringing around different places to make sure I got my hours in. There was no PHDU in Bradford so I had to do that in Leeds. A nursery placement was also arranged. For every placement outside my own area, I had to have a police check. Thankfully the course paid for it, but each time I had to wait for the results.

The list of assignments and competencies had me crying, there were pages and pages of them, several for each placement. How could I fit all these in , in such a short time ? They said if they overlap you can reuse some but to remember as you get further along the course more is expected in the content. I was overwhelmed.

I went through the booklet page by and listed them in a word format I could understand , they barely filled an A4 sheet, oh wow, that looks better, piece of cake !

After completing the course, I once again hoped for a promotion and asked about an E grade but was told once again if I won't go full time there was no promotion, I said I would go look elsewhere as I couldn't justify all these years, lots of extended roles, and now a paediatric nurse staying where I was. He told me I would never leave, he said I was bluffing

I loved my job and would have been ecstatic to run the paediatric area as a junior sister but it wasn't to be I guess and so I owed it to myself now to look for something else.

I was offered a job on the paediatric surgical ward, an E grade post I asked about giving my notice and was told I didn't need to as it was classed as a transfer; I was told I could be there within weeks and most certainly in the new year. I have to say I was a little disappointed as I so wanted to put the letter   in the ward managers Christmas card.

My first shift on the surgical ward I was looking after four children who had ENT surgery, they were all in adjacent beds so easy to keep an eye on, after the initial post op period it was basically feed and water them and attend to any necessary cares. one mum asked me to sit with her daughter while she went for a coffee, so there I was, watching Home and Away while a toddler slept and was getting paid way more than running around like a headless chicken in the A and E department.

It was around this time the A and E manager came to see me and asked if I would consider going back if they were to give me the E grade I had wanted for years, I told him it was too late and now I know how the other half live It would be unlikely I would change my mind, I did offer to do the odd overtime bank shift if they were stuck though, just to keep my hand in .

I worked on paediatric surgery for around six years before I moved to Hull.

Chapter Eight: The Great Escape

I had not told the kids what was happening at first, they thought we were going on holiday and were really excited. On the way I told them we were moving out and gave them a brief explanation. They must have heard what was going on as it wasn't an isolated outburst but was the worst.

We arrived at Angela's house early in the morning. They were all getting ready for work. Matthew her son tried to cheer the kids up and turned on the Christmas tree for them. I contacted my mum to let her know what happened and she said she will look for helplines etc., to be fair she was relieved I had left him, since the day she moved out she hated me being there with him but knew I needed to do it for myself.

I tried to use Angela's phone but it was dead. I didn't understand it because it was working earlier. I later found out the plug for the phone Was unplugged to plug in the Christmas tree...oops!

My mobile was pay as you go with limited minutes left. I called Nigel to tell him what happened as we were supposed to be meeting that day, I told him I couldn't as I had to find somewhere safe to go with the kids. he said he would help me if he could in any way. He transferred some credit onto my phone which enabled me to contact helplines and let everyone know what was happening. I wanted to tell people as I didn't want to have an excuse to go back and the more people that knew the better the support would be.

I called My Ex's dad to tell them as we were expecting them later that day, they said they were sad but knew it was only a matter of time, apparently, he had been really abusive with his first marriage too. They reassured me they would be there if I needed anything and to let them know once I knew what I was doing.

I telephoned work and told them what had happened and explained I had no idea if and when I would be back. They were very understanding and gave me two weeks emergency leave to sort myself out and that if I needed more, I should perhaps get a sick note.

When it got to lunchtime the kids were moaning, they were hungry and I felt bad enough imposing on Angela without raiding her fridge so I phoned Mick and asked him to get us some food. He went to MacDonald's which pleased the kids. I forgot to order something for myself but to be honest I was high on adrenaline and felt quite sick anyway.

Mum gave me the telephone number of women's aid who had refuges for women in crisis. I called them and they arranged for me to go to a refuge in Halifax. I was told I could only go if a woman could take me before the staff went home at 4 and that men were not allowed to even know where it was. That ruled Nigel out to take us, or my brother who had also offered. Angela was still at work so I phoned Joyce and she agreed to take me.

When we arrived at the refuge, we were given a quick tour and shown to a room. It was pretty overwhelming and the staff said they would do a proper induction the next day. They gave me a plastic cup each with teabags, coffee, sugar and milk... emergency supplies! I went to the local shop and bought food for tea, rushing to get back in case anyone saw me.

The room looked clean, it had bunk beds and a separate single bed. Nathan bagged the top bunk and Tiffany had the bottom bunk. As she got into bed, she noticed something between the slats under the top bunk...a used sanitary towel...nice!

My phone was going constantly from about 5pm, My Ex calling and leaving messages asking where we were, saying how sorry he was and asking where we were, he was worried. I answered it to tell him I had left and that he should not try and find me, I told him I was in a women's refuge and that he had gone too far, he tried to apologize but I hung up. I didn't answer the phone again but instead turned it off. I managed to sleep a little because I was exhausted from the night before and in the morning the staff knocked on the door.

I was told the rules of the house:

1 Kids in room before 9

2 There was a cleaning Rota

3 I had to pay rent but should get housing benefit

4 The address is secret, a PO box for correspondence

5 No men allowed near or on the property

6 only one Taxi firm is authorized

7 Children have to be supervised at all times

8 No childminders allowed on site

So, I had a few issues:

1, Tiff goes to bed at 8 and Nathan at 10, if they go together, they keep each other awake. They agreed to let me keep Nathan out as long as he was with me.

2. The cleaning Rota was great except eventually I had to go to work and the others in the house undid everything I had done before going to work. They agreed to let me have the bathroom close to our room which I was happy to keep clean. We cleaned up after ourselves in communal areas

3 I had to pay rent for Nathan as he was over 11 years old, yet he shared a room with us, so they agreed to giving me an L shaped bigger room which had an open plan bedroom for Nathan. I wasn't entitled to housing benefit because I worked. The fact I was off sick and on basic pay with a mortgage didn't count apparently so I paid £111 a week to stay there, however the housing office paid for Nathan's rent.

4. Understandable, however everybody in the area knew where it was anyway.

5 Daniel could not visit. If I wanted to see him, we had to see him away from the house

6 Difficult when they are limited and it takes 40 minutes to get back from shopping

7 I have no issue with this, I only wish the other women there had the same rule

8 I had to walk 30 minutes to nearest childminder because I wasn't allowed to let Nathan look after Tiffany for an hour before school. So, we left at 6 and I then travelled an hour and half to work every morning and Tiffany had to walk the half hour back for school which was local to the refuge. Nathan wasn't supposed to be in the house alone before school but as the staff didn't arrive until 9, he would be out before 8 anyway.

I was feeling defeated and also felt I was wasting a space in the refuge, there were women there battered and bruised and I was there because he trashed the kitchen ! The staff reassured me I had just as much right to be there as anyone else and abuse comes in many forms, I knew that from my safeguarding training but in the back of my mind I still had the thought it was my fault and trying to think what I could have done differently. "Did you know on average a woman will go back six times before she leaves for good ?" she said.

"Not me, it took a huge amount to make me leave and I will not be going back, I had it planned but just not yet. Maybe I stayed the 6 times where I should have left , who knows ?"

The first few days were crazy, there are certain things that have to be done from a legal perspective that I was not aware of, this was where the Refuge staff came in the most useful.

I was given a list of people I needed to contact and places I needed to visit, starting with a visit to the housing office about the rent...oh yeah, they got their priorities right. They told me to go into town with very brief instructions. Although I did my nurse training in Halifax years before, it had changed and I didn't know the area very well and asked about a bus to get there. I was told its quicker to walk, maybe ten minutes down the road but that was a 40-minute walk for me. I told them I was afraid as my husband works at all different places and could be anywhere, they just said if I had concerns while out, I should call the police. I walked into town with the kids just to be told I wasn't entitled to anything. They asked for all kinds of evidence such as 3 consecutive pay slips but as mine were all different they kept rejecting them, something to consider if you work odd shift patterns.

The initial pay slips were higher because they contained all the unsocial hours, but now I was off sick so my pay would be a lot less and I would only be returning to basic hours anyway due to child care issues.

I had several attempts at giving them the documentation they asked for, I would go into the office and hand it in, only to have it followed up with a letter the next day saying they required something else. In the end I went in with a carrier bag full of papers, I tipped it out on the desk and told them to take what they needed and I would come back for the rest. It was exhausting, all the time I had debt building up just to keep my head above water. I still never got housing benefit for me, only for Nathan.

Next came the tax credit office. I called there and explained what had happened. They said they needed to change my allowance from dual parent to single parent which was a significant difference. I was told I would get over £400 a month (That was more than my ex gave me for housekeeping money). However, the guy dealing with it made a small error, he put the application in for single parent allowance before cancelling the dual parent allowance sending the computer into confusion, as if I was committing fraud. They explained what had happened and gave me a giro for that month explaining it would rectify by next month. But this continued into the new year. Don't worry they said we will continue paying direct and in the new tax year we can correct it. In April the money was paid into my bank but in may I got a letter telling me I was not entitled to it and they wanted it back, they stopped paying me. I went to the tax office again and was told it's a computer error and I should ignore it; they gave me a giro. I didn't get anything then for a few months then got a giro for over 1,000. Then another letter a few months later saying I had to pay it back.

This involuntary saving scheme continued for about 3 years finishing with a bill for over £6,000 delivered on Christmas eve, " Bah Humbug !". I phoned the helpline and was told yes, I had to pay it back, I appealed but heard nothing. In the end I wrote an email to my local MP and he sorted it out for me, he said the computer was chucking out the demands and stopping my payments, I was entitled to everything and ignore the letters, the helpline used the same computer so had the same error and information. He said if I hear any more then contact him direct. I have never heard anything since and that was more than 13 years ago!

I was advised to get a sick note for at least six weeks so I went to the doctor who marked it as 'relocation stress' ha-ha yeah something like that. I saw another doctor at the practice when I started having swelling to my legs and she was so patronizing and told me it was my age. She offered me anti-depressants, I said " will that stop my legs swelling, make me find somewhere to live and keep me safe ? " She said "No" so I said I would be better with a clear head to sort my life out.

I am pretty sure the condescending attitude was because I lived at a PO box. I wrote to the FPC to complain and got a new GP. It seemed everywhere I went I was judged, not for anything I had done or said but because I was living in a refuge with my children. I was a vulnerable adult and the fact professional people would look down their nose at me still infuriates me.

I was advised to see a solicitor to commence divorce or separation proceedings. I was told I was entitled to legal aid because of the abuse but I had to agree to try counseling first. My Ex surprisingly agreed and we went to a meeting with the legal aid team. My Ex did not like the fact they were in control and stormed out. The result was me being granted legal aid as I was willing, and his behaviour was unacceptable. I filed for divorce straight away.

The papers were drawn up and sent to My Ex and he said he would not sign them. He was still convinced it was a temporary glitch. They sent them with a registered delivery and he still didn't sign them. They then sent them with a court bailiff who handed the papers to him, still no signature. As it was no longer straightforward it took 2 years instead of the 6 months I had been quoted. In the end the court granted a divorce without him.

Tiffany was settled into the local Catholic primary school within days, they even had a uniform for her to wear. It wasn't so easy for Nathan however and he was out of school for months. He had lots of time walking the streets and hanging out with other kids out of school. When he did get a place in school the problems started, he was staying off or getting into fights and trouble at school. I had gone back to work and I was getting calls all the time.

Time at the refuge was grim to say the least, I was sharing a house with some women I wouldn't normally let near my house. There were some really nice women there, genuinely in need of a refuge but also some who used it as a holiday camp, one woman said she came back regularly , just to get the grant and new clothes for her children. I got fed up of cleaning up after other people and feeding other people's kids.

I tried to cook in batches as it saved money and I had a freezer so could store food for when money was at its tightest. I seemed to be one of the few in there who actually cooked. If I made a pasta dish or stew the other kids would come sit at the table like I was the house caterer and I could never send a child away hungry even if I knew the mother had spent all day in the bookies and come home with new designer jeans she bought with her extra allowance, while her child got a free nursery place because he was vulnerable.

Nathan and Tiffany would play with the other kids but one kid was horrible and they refused to play with him. His mother went crazy accusing them of singling him out, bullying him, he was only

3 and my kids were 7 and 11 by then, I explained they didn't have to play with him if they didn't want to, after all he was virtually a baby to them.

One time I was called to the office for an important call and this woman left her kid in the kitchen while Tiffany was watching the stove for me. Her kid climbed on the worktop and was walking across the units to the cooker. Tiffany lifted him down and he started screaming, his mother rushed in and accused Tiff of hurting him, she tried to explain but the woman went berserk. Tiffany was heartbroken the staff came in and I told them I was not there to feed him and my children are not there to babysit her child, she tried to say he was not alone and she did supervise him, at that moment he climbed onto a highchair table and it fell over. A member of staff caught him. I said I rest my case and walked out.

There were a lot of parties and outings over the Christmas period , the kids got lots of gifts from various charities and Tiff actually said it was the best Christmas ever, at one point I had to agree , there was very little tension and we had our own space at the end of the day.

At Christmas I went to stay with Mum for a

few days to give us a sense of normality. When we returned the staff called me to the office. They said this same woman who had accused Tiff of hurting her son had invited a man to her room and her son had been wandering around the house for hours during the night. One of the residents had taken a video and informed them, apparently the woman was convinced I was the grass and said was going to kill me , I asked if they were throwing her out and they said no because her son is vulnerable, yeah ok. They just warned me to watch my back. I told them to stop worrying she doesn't scare me, I just knocked on her door and told her to bring it on, she reckoned she had no clue what I was talking about lol.

The New Year's Eve party was the best, the staff had left supplies for us and a couple of the girls bought extra alcohol. I even tried my first spliff but I was that pissed I doubt it had any effect except make me cough. It amused the kids though, everyone who phoned to wish me happy new year were informed by the kids I was smoking weed, I had one drag ffs   and nearly choked to death !!

One night the fire alarm went off, the staff would go home in the evening so weren't there to supervise. I called the helpline and they just said they didn't need to come and to just get everyone out and wait for fire brigade. We all evacuated the house and were sat outside. It was cold and wet; the kids were complaining they were cold. One of the women went back inside to get blankets and cushions for the kids, then went back for her coat, then for a nappy for her baby, then went and made a coffee asking if anyone else wanted one, then another woman went back in to put on a sexy negligee (In December !) she said If there were sexy firemen she wanted to be prepared, I couldn't believe what was happening. I told them they shouldn't keep going in it was dangerous, only to be told it is ok it isn't a fire. Apparently one of them had been smoking a joint and to get rid of smell had sprayed body spray around the room, this had set the smoke alarm off. It was too ridiculous to be funny at the time. The firemen inspected the house and said someone had been over keen with spray and to be more careful next time. I cried laughing as we went back inside.

On Mother's Day I asked the kids to come to church with me, I promised to take them to the park afterwards. When we got back, they refused to get changed into more suitable clothes so I told them they couldn't go to the park. About half hour later two of the other women , high on weed knocked on the door, told the kids they would take them if I wouldn't and they just walked out of the door without a word, I was devastated, it was the worst Mother's Day ever !

I started to feel just as much at risk there as I ever did at home, I felt I was losing the grip on my own children, they were picking up bad habits, one girl in there used to hit her mother and she just let her. I warned my kids they wouldn't get away with it so not to try !

Cars would park across the street selling drugs, even Tiffany knew why they were there, she told me as I joked one day " hey, go get me a 99 cone from the ice cream van, I assume it is ice cream he is selling as there are that many kids going to him "

I was desperate to move out. I really needed to get some normality back. I was high priority on the housing waiting list but told that could be months. After about 4 months I had enough of waiting for housing and decided to rent privately. The staff tried to put me off but when I told them I pay £111 a month for a room there, and I can pay

£375 rent for a house with three bedrooms they backed off. I didn't get any help with moving and used my credit card to buy everything from scratch. We moved into the house with 4 cups a kettle and a pack of teabags. I bought bean bags for seats and had the kids mattresses brought from home.

So many women got grants and financial support when moving out, help with a new start but because I was working, I was not entitled to anything. This seemed so wrong because at the time my wage was paying for the rent in the refuge, extra costs of child care and also the mortgage to stop the house from being repossessed before we sold it. I had tried to pay interest only but the bank said you can only do that after you are in arrears

The staff had advised me to quit my job when I first went to the refuge as I would be better off but it was all I had left. I loved my job and needed to keep a certain level of normality in my life. When I realised how much I missed out on financially it might have been a good time to take a career break.

The day after I moved into the rented house, I took my credit card on a shopping spree. I was stopped three times that day and had to confirm my ID as I was spending more than usual on it lol. I explained I needed everything for a new home and they backed off. It was great until I had to start paying for it. With a mortgage, rent, child care costs and credit card bills it was hard. My pay had gone down as I had to work basic hours to accommodate child care.

Once we settled into our house, I could go back to working shifts and Nathan agreed to look after Tiffany it seemed ideal but I was unaware that by this time Nathan had got in with the local Borstal bait, there had been so much going on I had not noticed.

I will never understand the hold this boy had on Nathan but for some reason this kid had Nathan totally under his control. Nathan started stealing and taking my credit and debit cards to the local Tesco to buy crap. He learnt that you don't need to sign under £25 at self-serve and the cards didn't need pin confirmation either. I only realised when my bill came in and it was itemized as totally random stuff: A crystal making kit, pringles, snacks, toys etc. I went into Tesco to ask if it was customary to serve a child of 13 who looked ten with a gold card. They said they only check ID if they buy things that need age identification, after all some parents send the kids to the shop when they can't go themselves and basically, I should look after my card better!

I came home one day to a letter from the police saying Nathan had been throwing eggs at cars and had even thrown them at a police car, the letter was asked me to speak to him about it and tell him how dangerous it was. What was happening to him ? Why was he being like this when he knew I was struggling ? Daniel was so mad with him too and told him he didn't realise what I had saved him from and he should be treating me better.

I told Nathan's Dad what he had been up, I thought maybe a stern word from him may help but instead he pretty much said I took him so he was my problem.

Nathan was staying off school and leaving school whenever he wanted to hang out with his new friend. He was leaving the basement window open before leaving for school and coming back after I left for work. Between the two of them (I am assuming there was no one else involved) they stole all my DVD's, music CD's and Jewellery. I took Nathan into the police station and told them what was happening, they gave Nathan a stern talking to but said I could not prove this boy took stuff and if he was invited in with Nathan then basically, he could have been given the stuff. If I was willing to give Nathan criminal record, I could proceed but they advised against it.

I bought a padlock for a cupboard in the loft to make a secure place to leave things but this kid taught him how to break the lock on the door without it being detected and without opening the padlock. A lot more went missing before I realised what he had done.

I was so angry with Nathan, I sent him to stay with my mum while I could figure out my next move. I contacted social services and told them I wasn't coping and needed help. I explained I was on my own and this boy had total control over Nathan, Even If I took him to school he walked out. They said he was in a safe place now so they couldn't help me. I told them my mum lived in sheltered housing and he wasn't allowed to stay with her long term. I asked if I had to physically hurt him to get support, then I would lose my daughter, my job and possibly my home just because they wouldn't help, they agreed to come and see me the next day.

Nathan was allocated a social worker. She

came every Thursday and took Nathan on a nice little outing. They thought by showing him the nice things he could be doing he wouldn't want to do the bad stuff, how naïve the system is, don't they realise he has just come from middle class suburbia and this new and exciting life was more appealing to him?

Tiffany was really mad, she said why should she go to school and be good when he is such a knob head and gets taken out of school on trips...fair point!

Nathan persuaded the social worker to take him to the local Games Workshop, he didn't tell her he went there virtually every day and was obsessed with Warhammer and had been for years. Nathan had collected a few armies and spent a lot of time over the years painting them and studying strategies. He told the social worker that they had to pay £5 to hire an army at the shop so she gave him the £5 as requested, he already had his own army there that he stored behind the counter, so he got that and pocketed the fiver. Nathan couldn't wait to tell me when he got home.

When I told the social worker what he had done she just said maybe it wasn't working and cancelled the support. I told her that isn't what I meant; I meant the path they were taking wasn't helping. I don't think she liked the fact she had been outsmarted. A few days later I got a letter saying I was refusing help...err no not quite! I guess it was easier for her to say that to her seniors than admit she had been taken for a ride by a 13-year-old. I telephoned them to tell them I had not refused help and initially I was hoping for some kind of respite while we sorted our future out. I was told they had nothing else to offer so once again I was on my own.

I tried to keep Nathan in the house but I had to go to work to keep paying the bills. I relied on the unsocial pay to make ends meet. I came home from work one afternoon and Nathan was in the house drinking beer. There was another boy from school with him. I phoned school to ask why I was not informed he had left and they stated he was in school. I told them he was in front of me and they still "assured" me he was there. I asked to speak to the headmaster and she hung up!

Nathan said he had been put in isolation so when the teacher went to the toilet he just walked out, bringing another kid with him. As far as school was concerned the register was ticked so it wasn't their problem.

After this I contacted the school and went in to see the head, I told them what happened and instead of apologising they decided to suspend him. Basically, saying they couldn't keep him there so he may as well stay home. They didn't give him any work to do either and after missing so much school I really worried about his future education.

I contacted the department of education who told me they had been informed I had told the school I wanted to home school him. I said this was not true and voiced my concerns over his education , I was advised it could take months to get another place in school, still no work was given to him. This was in the first year of his GCSE's.

Even though I kept Nathan in as much as possible when he wasn't in school ,the boy he had been hanging around with was always skulking around the house, he would shout threats through the letterbox and throw things at the windows, he even broke a window at one point.

The police were involved at that time and they asked if I wanted to have him arrested or given a warning, I told them all I wanted was for us to be left alone to get on with life. When they tried to talk to him, he became aggressive towards the police , they came back and told me he 'failed the attitude' test so they were going to arrest him anyway.

The boy would continue to come to the house when I was at work and brag to Nathan how he had been able to go on a mechanic course and taken abseiling etc. compliments of the justice system, not the kind of incentive to keep a yob out of trouble.

Not being in school just made things worse, Nathan started glue sniffing and inhaling aerosol. I was losing my boy and nobody seemed to care. I took him to see the GP who referred him to CAMHS. They didn't really offer any support and I felt defeated. I decided the best thing was to move him away from Halifax and give us all a chance of a fresh start.

The house had been sold by now and I had enough for a deposit in the bank.

Now was the time to start over.

Chapter Nine: A whole new start

I wasn't sure of where to go; I couldn't move back to Bradford as I was afraid that My Ex could turn up on my doorstep drunk one morning and start threatening me.

Things with Nigel had cooled off as he was not showing any signs of joining us, I didn't blame him, after all I was the one who said I would never leave home for him. The last thing I wanted was to become someone's booty call so moving near him was out of the question.

I even considered emigrating at one point, as a dual qualified staff nurse the world was my oyster. I was offered a really nice settlement in Canada, free child care and free accommodation for 6 months and all expenses paid to transfer. I was given a DVD that showed all the wonderful things we could enjoy, it seemed like a really good idea, the kids were buzzing.

I told Mum of my plans and she broke down, she was afraid she would never see us again and reminded me I had a new granddaughter to consider, in the end I felt so bad I abandoned the idea.

We looked at housing in the Lake district where my Friend Jane lived but there wasn't really much in my price bracket other than a terrace house with no garden.

I would also need a job, there weren't many that were easily accessible, although Jane offered me a job as her carer, I didn't really want to cross that barrier, she was a great friend and confidante but wiping her bum felt like crossing the line. Now if it had been a job as a companion I would have jumped at the chance.

Daniel was still living in Hull with his girlfriend and my granddaughter, I figured it made sense to look for something near there. I would see more of them and I could commute for work until I found a job in Hull and the kids could come back with me to Bradford each time and stay with my mum while I was at work.

I found a nice house, an end terrace near all the amenities with a local bus route to virtually anywhere. The local schools looked good too, Daniel and his wife agreed to stay at my house with my granddaughter while I commuted so it would make it easier. My boss said they would keep my shifts condensed so it meant I was only away from home 2 nights a week. I also applied for jobs in Hull because realistically the commute was not suitable for long term.

I saved some money back from the house sale to give the kids a holiday, we discussed the choices and decided on a short holiday abroad, Disneyland Paris on a coach trip, and a 2-week holiday in the UK where mum could join us too. Mum didn't have a passport and did not want to go abroad, she said she didn't trust the doctors and she was too old to take the risk. We all had passports from when we went to France so that was good for us.

I booked a 2-week holiday in a Skegness holiday camp. BIG mistake !. The place was a dump. After a 6 ½ hour coach ride we arrived there and were told our apartment was at the other side of the camp, we couldn't book in for two hours but they reckoned it would take an hour to get over there so they said it wasn't worth storing our luggage. I asked if we could have some help to get there but they just shrugged and said " take your time"

We walked over to the other side stopping for lunch on the way , by then I had a migraine, the kids were complaining about dragging their cases and mum was on the verge of a heart attack. Then we found out the apartment was on the third floor, Mum started to cry and said she couldn't make it. I telephoned the rep and told them we were not happy; we had asked for somewhere with easy access and had told them about mums heart trouble and my walking difficulties. I said if they could not accommodate this, I wanted a refund and we would find somewhere in Skegness to stay. Within minutes they sent a kind of golf cart to take us to a different apartment. At first glance it looked good but on closer inspection it was filthy. The bin had a funky smell and when we lifted out the bin bag it was full of cigarette ends and mouldy food. The apartment was in the non-smoking area too !

The kids wanted to go swimming in the afternoon , mum went for a lie down so I packed a swim bag and walked back to the main complex. When we got there, it was under 12's only. Nathan was 13 but looked younger so I said he could go if he wanted but he said he better not in case they found out, he didn't want to get me into trouble. Tiff went in on her own while we had a drink upstairs.

There were two pools that we could see, several members of staff were there to supervise and there were floats and inflatables for the to use,

Tiffany was in one of the pools with some girls and then I looked in the other pool, there was a man, yes, a man, an Asian man with a beard, maybe in his twenties, he had a surf board over himself but from where we sat, we could tell he was wanking. As the young girls went past, he was touching them, even though they screamed the staff were too busy talking to each other to notice, I felt sick. I went downstairs and told Tiffany to get out and alerted a member of staff. The response was " oh well, they are getting out now ". I said "how did he manage to get in ? he had a beard and mustache for fucks sake !" I was told they don't check the birth certificate !

The next time Tiffany went swimming with the under 12's she went in with Nathan, I had gone to the launderette with mum. Apparently, she slipped on the floor and banged her head, when she got back into the pool she went into the 'rapids' and passed out. She was taken out of the pool and when she came round, she told them where we were. They brought her to the launderette and she was deathly pale. I was told she had been sick about 4 times but if she gets worse to let them know . Tiffany started vomiting in the bin so we abandoned the washing and took her back to the apartment. Tiffany did not want to go to the hospital and I figured as a paediatric nurse I may as well observe her for 24 hours as let her go to a ward where some poor nurse that has 5 other kids to look after, does the same. She improved overnight but I didn't let her go without me after that. They didn't even tell Nathan and he came back later in tears afraid he had lost his sister.

I was under the impression that once inside everything was free but there was very little there for the older kids to do that was free , maybe a couple of rides in their age range but even they got boring after a couple of days, Things like the laser quest and cinema you had to pay extra for, but I spent nearly £2000 on the holiday so I didn't expect to have to pay for activities too.

There was an 'exclusive' beach there so we decided to give that a go , it was rowdy and full of unsavoury characters, we had been there a few minutes when some guy shouted " Oy come back here ya little c*nt !" to a child who looked about 2 or 3 years old. The look on mum's face was a picture, don't get me wrong I can swear with the best of them but there are times when you have to be a little careful. A family beach is one of those places IMO. We packed up our stuff and left.

Everywhere you went there were queue's, if you wanted to see a show, you started queueing at 4 to go in at 6 and the shows started at 7, we went to one that was pretty mediocre and standing room only so we didn't bother again.

The mealtimes were a joke too, the queues were miles long in the canteen style café. We opted for the more expensive a la carte restaurant instead, we ate there a couple of times, the food was nice in there but I couldn't afford that every day.

After such a crap start, we went on the free shuttle bus through to Skegness for the rest of the days and just used the holiday camp as a base.

I put in a complaint when we got home and they sent me a £25 off voucher as compensation.... No thanks I won't be back !

Things seemed to go back to normal we had our own house and I was far enough away to actually feel safe. I managed to get Tiffany in School straight away, but it was much harder for Nathan, he was in senior school and the places were limited, either that or his reputation preceded him. Nathan's behaviour continued to be challenging and once again he was referred to CAMHS for support. He would skip appointments but when I offered to take him the staff said he has to want to come. Do they not realise he was referred to them because he makes BAD choices?

Nathan eventually managed to get a place in school and his behaviour improved a little. The teachers seemed more invested into helping him and he managed to catch up on his GCSE work. Nathan even got the headmasters award for achievement which shocked me a little.

I was working on the agency in Hull on a more frequent basis so I handed my notice in at BRI. I applied for a job on the paediatric ward and was accepted. The job was on the medical ward though and not surgery. I was in a "beggars can't be choosers" situation so I accepted it.

I never felt welcome on the ward, I don't know if I took someone else's job or just that I was an outsider, I hated it, I cried going to work and I cried going home. I didn't really make any friends initially and on the odd occasion I joined them for a ward night out I was ostracized. I did make a couple of friends after a while and a couple of nurses were quite supportive but my shifts seemed to fall different to theirs. I tried to swap wards but was told there wasn't an opening, I had heard there was a nurse on the surgical ward who wanted medicine , I suggested a swap but was told they didn't want her on their ward !

I did say I found the night shifts hard as a single parent to the person doing the off duty and I was told "We all have to work our share; you knew what the job was when you applied " so I worked virtually half my shifts on nights. It was hard because I hated leaving them home alone overnight, technically I was not allowed to leave them together but I had no choice, Daniel and his wife helped a lot even during those times.

I found out years later the person who said that to me apparently never worked nights as she was a single parent with a 14-year-old !.

One night shift I was looking after a very sick baby, the other two nurses on duty were relatively junior but seemed competent. I asked them to look after my other two children as things were getting bad for the baby, I asked the doctors to transfer the baby to PHDU but they refused, I was genuinely worried. The next morning while we were in handover the baby was transferred to PHDU after a senior review.

After handover I was summoned to the office. The two nurses had complained I had left them unsupported and not even done any observations on my own children. I explained the situation and said I thought if I asked them to look after my children they would or tell me why not , I didn't think I needed to check. I was told I should have re allocated the baby to one of them and I said if I had he would have been dead in the morning. He said maybe I needed more support as I was from another trust and they work differently there.

The next night shift I was asked by a junior nurse for details on my patients so she could hand over . I said I would hand over and she replied she had been told I wasn't allowed. When it came time for break instead of leaving me with an auxiliary a nurse came from another department to cover the break. She asked why I wasn't allowed to be on my own , I didn't know it was the first I heard of it.

In the morning I approached the ward manager and I was livid, he said it was a misunderstanding and he doesn't know where the information came from. It turned out two of his staff had been looking at my online record and told everyone I had to be supervised at all times. The manager stated when he wrote that it was before our chat and he had since realised what I was capable of. The place was one of the biggest cliques I had ever come across in my whole nursing career. I cannot understand why no one was disciplined about the breach of confidentiality, although one of the nurses did apologise afterwards.

When I left Bradford, I was a well-respected member of the team, probably next in line for a promotion and here they made me feel like I had just qualified or landed from another planet. It isn't as if they were more advanced because most of the equipment, they had I hadn't seen since the 1980's. They even had a bed pan washer for goodness's sake, they weren't using bedpan liners just the old metal bedpans ! Patient care came secondary to paperwork and it was every man for himself when things went wrong.

Nathan continued to cause problems and now he was getting older he became harder to control. He would have outbursts and destroy things, he stole things and he made us feel like we were walking on eggshells all the time, I actually felt I was back with his dad some days it was that bad. In the end after a particularly destructive outburst, I threw him out, he wasn't attending college and he didn't have a job, he was 17 so I had no financial income for him so why was I expected to keep him and pay for all the damage he caused. He was on some kind of youth course that day and I received a call from one of the youth workers, he said Nathan had told him what happened and said he was afraid to come home, was he ok to return, I said "no, I threw him out, I can't afford to keep him anymore".

Nathan was placed in a hostel and Arrangements were made for family counselling. I loved my son and wanted things to get back to normal, but I needed to be sure I felt safe at home . At the appointments We were asked what we could do to improve things and Nathan stated it was all him, we had done nothing wrong and he deserved to be kicked out. I explained the bills were higher because of him and the stealing and property damage were becoming too much for me to handle. I told them he smokes and I cannot afford to pay for his habit. I told them he has no income at all and it was unrealistic to expect me to pay for everything. As he was under 18, he was not entitled to any benefits, but being out of education I no longer got child benefit

Nathan agreed to a set of basic house rules and Daniel wrote up a contract for him. He was given an allowance by social care to cover his cigarette money and a little spending money, and I was to be paid £35 a week to cover his costs if I agreed to let him come home. I still think it was the best decision to kick him out as he learnt what he would be missing out on but I was happy he was coming home again.

Things really settled down after that, Nathan was approached in the unemployment office and enrolled on a course by One Hull for Kids out of Education and employment, He even took part in the Clipper race as a Hull Ambassador at 18 sailing from Qingdao to California. It changed his life completely and I really appreciate what they did for him.

Mum & Nathan at the start of Clipper Race

Nathan contacted his dad to tell him and he was so pleased, he actually thought he would make his dad proud, instead his dad just brushed it off and asked to speak to me. He said that this had gone on long enough and we should get back together , he said if he couldn't have me, he didn't want my kids either and that was the last time Nathan spoke to him for over ten years. He had spent half his life trying to please his dad , at last he had achieved something amazing and got no praise or recognition for it, I could see how disappointed he was.

I started to see a lot more of Nigel and he was so supportive, he arranged for us to go to California to meet the boat, it was a trip of a lifetime, we stayed with my cousin for a couple of weeks in Los Angeles, with a one-week trip to San Francisco in the middle to go meet the boat and see the sights . I actually got to go to the Snoopy theme park, Knotts Berry Farm which was way better than Disney IMO.

Waiting in line for one of the rides I spotted Snoopy walking around, I said "I have to go get my photo taken with Snoopy" and started to go back down the line, Tiff was like" you do know it's a spotty kid in a suit I assume"

" Oh, shatter my dreams why don't you !, anyway, so is Mickey mouse and You ran to get a photo with him the day before ! "

Tiffany was such a brat in California, she

had the " You are not my dad" syndrome the whole time. She said she never asked to go and didn't really see what an opportunity it was. It must have been so hurtful for Nigel but he still stayed calm and did his best to ignore it. I could see he wasn't ready for the step father role in the present climate. I just wish my kids could see him as I saw him and not as the enemy.

Sitting under the Golden Gate Bridge waiting for the 'Ull and 'Umber was one of the proudest moments of my life, although it was also one of the dumbest for me. The boat was running late and we weren't sure if it was going to come that night. I called the helpline to ask for an update. I wanted to make sure we were in the right place.

" Where are you ?" he asked

" Under the Humber Bridge " I said like a prat.

Nigel still laughs every time he sees the Bridge on TV " oh look, it's the Humber Bridge , ha ha de har"

" Sod off !"

Meeting Nathan in San Francisco after the race

Back in Hull things were starting to change. After 3 years on the medical ward, I was given the opportunity to change to the surgical ward. It was like I had come home. The team were so welcoming and supportive. I settled in really easily and for the first time since I left home, I felt I belonged.

On my first shift someone asked if I needed any help, that was the first time anyone had said that in 3 years, I almost cried. The staff on the ward worked so well together as a team.

My relationship with Nigel was difficult and I really wanted him to move in with me. He had commitments at home and needed to support his mum so initially it was not practical. Nigel spent a lot of time with us and after his mum died, he moved in permanently. The kids weren't too keen on the new man in the house and played up quite a lot testing him and me but eventually they realised he was there for the duration and he was one of the good guys.

The children were older now and Nigel didn't have to take on the step dad role. I think they both knew that they had a good set up here and as adults we were under no obligation to provide a roof over their heads , I am sure they knew that.

Tiffany moved out when she as 19 and Nathan stayed for a lot longer, apart from the mess in his room everyone seemed to get along fine and now he owns his own house nearby and is working in a Games shop doing what he loves.

Chapter Ten: Online Friendships

When the children were young, we never had a computer, I wouldn't even know where to start with one but when Daniel went to school, they told me he was a whizz on the computer and he would really benefit from having one at home.

I looked in the local paper and saw a few for sale, we couldn't afford to buy a new one but I could run to a second hand one.

The Amstrad seemed to be the most popular so I went ahead and bought one, I had no clue that the reason there were so many for sale is because they were becoming obsolete and in fact windows was the way to go.

We got an instruction book which had instructions of how to input information to make games etc and you could buy tapes with programmes already on them too. I think if I remember correctly the memory on the whole machine was about 500 mb which you could increase up to I Gb with an additional drive. The storage was on floppy disc which on the model we had wasn't even built in we had to buy a separate disc drive. I used an old tape player for the games which would scream as they loaded ha-ha, the internet was the same at that stage, screeching to get a dial up connection. It is a sound that haunts you forever.

When we realised how shit the computer was, we looked at buying something better. Nathan was still quite young so we bought a computer as a family gift rather than buying anything big, we bought a kind of kid's keyboard that went over the keyboard that had toddler games on it. I saw one of those in cash converters being sold as a kid's computer for £100, it was only £20 new from the toyshop, I told them but they didn't believe me and said they paid £60 for it, well done whoever sold it to them ha-ha.

We bought a brand new up to date computer, complete with windows and a load of games, by then I was so used to having to input everything when we got windows, I never understood why people thought it was complicated. having said that I had a word programme on there and was trying to type something, I didn't know why I couldn't get the drop-down menu. Daniel came over and said "you are pressing the wrong mouse button stupid" Stupid ?? my 11-year-old son called me stupid because I didn't know as much about computers as he did.

I went straight out and bought every computer magazine and went to library and read idiot books about computers. In the end I got pretty good at it. I even made a website with Yahoo GeoCities a free online web hosting.... not that kind of website, get your head out of the gutter!

My website had several pages, complete with links and everything. I joined the site fights, an online website competition, you had to choose a group and they all had their own logo image. I joined the Cherubs as they had the cutest picture of little Angels. I didn't know at the time it was like a religious based group. It didn't matter though everyone had their own site and the content was up to you. I had a page dedicated to Snoopy but I ended up with a nasty letter from UFS asking me to take it down or they would sue me so I lost that one pretty quick. I had a lot of topical pages; it was important to change with the seasons and keep up to date with items of interested. My Christmas page was full of links to online activities, recipes, fun for kids etc, I had an Easter page , a Halloween page and a page dedicated to My dead hamster: Is it dead or is it hibernating ? a page full of hamster facts and how to ensure you don't throw a hibernating hamster in the bin like I did, only to go back later to flick the cornflakes off when you realise you made a mistake (It was actually dead but I didn't know for sure , the vet said to put it somewhere warm and if it started to smell it was dead !).I became a dab hand at graphics too, I learnt to make animations with paint shop pro. I became a 'cheerleader'. Someone who visited other websites in the same group giving encouragement and leaving inspirational messages. It helped to keep people motivated when their website became stagnant. I needed a character so I made an animated Angel 'doll' called Angelica Hotwings, she was dressed in orange and black with wings and had flames around her feet. Her image was left in guestbooks everywhere.

My website ended up being the top of the Cherub group, I had a page full of virtual trophies and awards, it was entered into the top level of the competition, but came last out of five. I was disappointed at first then realised that meant I was 5th in the whole worldwide competition which was pretty awesome. To get to the top there were a lot of vote exchanges going on so to be fair it wasn't much of a competition unless you were there full-time swapping votes for votes!

I quit my website when GeoCities shut down, by then most web hosts charged for space or you had to do all the formatting from scratch and I really couldn't be bothered starting over.

I spent a lot of time online in the evenings especially when My ex was working away, I was home alone and the kids were in bed. I made quite a few friends; some I still have. You would put criteria in a search bar and find like-minded people to chat to. I searched for women, married, with photos, professional. My first friends were also nurses, we had a lot in common and would chat for hours. Jane was from Cumbria, it was like I had known her forever, we often put the world to rights, it always seemed easier to talk to people online than offline, after all you would probably never meet them.

I had talked about the issues from my childhood with the team leader from the site fights, I would get really distressed about it and she suggested I confide in someone closer to home, she was in America after all. I had never told anyone but somehow It felt like the right time. George was dead so he couldn't hurt me anymore. I hadn't even told my husband!

In the end I told Jane everything. At the time I still blamed myself. I felt dirty and cheap I told Jane I understood if she didn't believe me or never wanted to speak to me again but she was just the opposite, she reassured me it wasn't my fault and helped me come to terms with it. I felt such a sense of relief. We never discussed it again and I felt able to move forward,

Jane came to visit me a few times and it was like we had always known each other. I took the first work sickie of my life to go visit her once, my ex was going to the Lakes to look at a boat so I bummed a lift with him and went for lunch with Jane. We took Tiffany with us but the boys were in School.

I felt so guilty the next day I actually felt ill. I never understood how people could just chuck a sickie from work without a care in the world.

Just after I left home Jane had surgery, but there were complications and she ended up quadriplegic, at first, I didn't know how to handle it. How do you moan about your life to someone who is bedridden? Even when I went to see her in hospital, I was stuck for something to say "so what do you do for fun around here?" I asked as she lay in an ICU bed staring at the ceiling what kind of dumb thing was that to say? I felt terrible, but Jane being Jane answered "dunno I haven't decided yet "I felt kind of relieved she didn't tell me to get out.

The first few visits were hard, I felt like I lost my best friend, but as time went on, I realise it is the same Jane but her priorities are different now, we don't chat online every day but I cherish the times she was there right when I needed her. I love being in her company and sometimes wish I lived closer.

We try to visit the Lakes every year and love to spend time with Jane and her husband Bob when we are there. I still consider Jane as one of my best friends ever.

I also became friends online with Mags and her friends Jen and Lynne, we would often have a chat room going, I had a few random guys who would message me, sending dick pics and flirting, sometimes I would copy the messages they sent and paste them into the chat room. The four of us would decide on a response between us, making him believe I was getting excited while all the time we were using him for entertainment, I have never laughed so much in my life. Some poor guy at the other end getting off, while I sat at my end eating my toast and enjoying a cuppa tea.

Mags and Jen also came to visit us in Bradford and once again it is like you have known them all your life because you can really talk about anything with someone over a keyboard.

After I left home, I met Mags and her boys in Lanzarote for our first proper holiday, it was brilliant. I had never had a holiday abroad before other than the camping holiday, I wanted to go somewhere hot but I was wary of taking the children anywhere on my own. I had asked Mags for advice, she had booked a holiday and suggested we join them.

Mags advised me to say "stop" when they were pouring drinks, I was used to Optics behind the bar and 'measures' of spirits. I wondered why I felt so drunk with only a couple of drinks.

Walking to the bar there were glass walls on the pavement between the shops, you couldn't really see them as they were full of clothes, towels and bags etc. When we came back the glass walls had nothing on them, and I never knew they were there. I was talking on the phone and walked straight into one, I was a little stunned but just backed off and carried on walking. Mags and Tiffany were hysterical rolling around on the floor laughing until they cried.

Nathan would go to the disco with Mag's boys and we would go to Hooks bar and drink cocktails, choosing different ones each night until we completed the menu, Tiff would work her way through the non-alcoholic ones obviously!

Cocktails in Lanzarote

We were only there for one week and Mags was there for two, when we went home, we were all crying. we were so alike and we had such a good time that we met up again the following year but for two weeks that time. When we returned the glass walls had warning sign stickers on, which had us all laughing all over again, I wonder if they saw me on CCTV?

I had a few guys I would just chat to as friends too, Nigel was one of those, he was around most days and we just chatted like old friends. We would talk on cam and he was still at home with his wife as I was with My husband at the time. The kids would say hi and got used to him being around.

When he suggested we meet up I was hesitant at first but then why not? He was a friend, why should it be any different just because he was a man? I felt safe as I wasn't attracted to him so in the end I agreed.

I was aware of the sick people on the internet, I read about the catfish stories and people getting ripped off for money by men they believed they loved after chatting online. I had no money so that was never going to be an issue to be fair. I did chat to some guys who were unsavoury to say the least but I never had the desire to meet them and soon got to see the ugly side when things didn't go as they planned.

I had seen Nigel at home, I saw his family around him and they saw me, the same goes for him I guess, he had seen me in my natural environment too.

I made a list of house rules, no physical contact, I wouldn't get into his car and it was strictly as friends. We arranged to meet at the museum of Photography, I think it called the media museum or something now. I figured anyone from Bradford would be at work through the week and unlikely to visit the museum, I thought if I see anyone from work, I will say it is a relative and any relatives I will say it's a work colleague, no problem.

When we got inside the museum I saw kids, lots of kids on school trips, shit! did I sign any forms from school for my kids to go on a trip? I couldn't remember, but then I didn't recognise any of the uniforms so far anyway.

We had a wander around and then went to the Hilton for lunch, I had a wonderful time. I felt a real connection but convinced myself it was just like Mags and Jane, the feeling of always knowing someone, like meeting an old friend.

When it was time to say goodbye, I went one way and he went the other, we didn't hug, just said bye and parted, He did offer me a lift in his car but I declined, remember the rule! I jumped in a taxi and went to pick my kids up from school. Within seconds my phone went ping with a message from Nigel thanking me for a great day. I messaged back saying I had a great day too. I said it felt weird just parting like that, no hug or anything and he felt the same, it was a blunt end to the day.

We continued to chat on a daily basis, I enjoyed his company and I assume he enjoyed mine as he kept coming back.

The next time we met up it was in Halifax, we went for lunch and as we came out, he stopped me, "we have to get this hug out the way sometime" so we hugged and the next thing I knew we were kissing. I knew then my life had changed.

I had found a man that was beautiful on the inside and there was nothing anyone could say that would change my mind.

CHAPTER ELEVEN: THE CRAFTY HOARDER

I have always enjoyed crafting, I took art at school but didn't do that well at it, a few of my drawings were good but not *that* good.

It all got serious when I was in Halifax, I went to buy a birthday card and they all seemed so plain and boring, and not that cheap considering. I figured I could do better myself. It starts so small you don't know what is happening. I bought a card kit from the 99p shop, it had five cards to put together , the kit had everything you need, the cards, the envelopes, the little sticky pads and some tacky bits to stick on the front of each one. I was hooked, I went back and bought another kit the next day.

Once I had done a few I started looking online and on Pinterest for ideas, I bought more craft supplies and even designed some cards of my own. I designed one like a pair of jeans with a pocket to put money in, the denim was taken from a photo of my jeans and layered into a 3d effect. It got published in a magazine and I was thrilled. I got a huge stack of craft papers as a prize. My mum went out and bought a copy to show everyone and a copy for me . she stood in the supermarket showing anyone that walked past lol.

I have had a few designs published since but then I realised half of my designs were being reproduction by bigger brands, I even saw my jeans design on create and craft once being passed off as someone else's design, yes, I guess the concept could be thought of but I photographed my jeans to get the image !

My Jeans pocket card

I sent a card in the 'card for a celebrity' section of a card making magazine and won a bouquet of flowers. My card was a kid on a trike that said 'bon voyage', I made it potentially for Billy Connelly, I doubt he ever saw it though lol.

My best prize was a craft storage bag I got for sending a photograph of my crafty mess , I reckon most real crafters had a mess like mine, I doubt the desks and craft rooms have the neat and tidy desks you see on create and craft.

The prizes seemed to dry up as the card magazine focused on the Facebook page, asking people to share pictures of their cards with a chance to be featured in the magazine, no mention of a craft prize. I used to be on a craft forum and Someone said congratulations to me one day because she had seen another one of my cards on the readers page, I was puzzled because I hadn't sent one in for ages. She showed me a photo of the page. It was one I had shared on Facebook. I sent the editor a message and asked how come I didn't get notified or get a prize and they took my details; I got a small craft bundle a few days later. I wonder how many other people were featured that never knew.

Did you know that crafting and collecting craft supplies are two separate hobbies ? I do now.

In the beginning I hated using the good papers, I used to scan them and use copies, but now I have learnt the feel of good quality papers on a card make a huge difference so I use it

Nowadays people are offended if I buy a card and always expect a hand crafted one. I also have a handful of people who regularly order cards from me whilst others prefer the flat faced cards from the likes of Moon pig et al lol. I can do flat cards too but I prefer to make them interesting as well as personal.

My niece bought a card from moonpig once, she didn't change the names under the images, not realising it is a bot making them and it won't notice. When the card arrived, it had the photos she uploaded with totally random names underneath lol. If she had come to me, I would have messaged her saying " you do realise the sample names are on it ya plank ?" lol

Christmas can be a nightmare, over 100 cards I made a until last year, all hand crafted and majority unique, I got about 20 cards back, other than family cards, some looked like they came from the bottom of the box, a last-minute thing. Some the size   gift cards so I decided to reduce the ones I make, starting with work, I only made individual ones after that for those I actually saw outside work and made one big one for the ward.

I like to recycle cards and elements from cards too, so last year's Christmas cards will be next year's gift tags or card toppers. I don't like to throw away nice things. Every time mum sent me a card, she would say she had chosen certain ones because they had bits on, I could reuse, she was so thoughtful.

I can be a bit of a poet too; One Christmas I wrote a new version of Night before Christmas on the front of a huge Christmas card for the staff on the children's ward, for a few years after that it was expected of me . I think I have written about ten now.

You see , that is what happens when people discover you have a skill, they expect it all the time. I baked a cake once , after that I got

"Where is the cake ? " Virtually every shift

When I decided to start making cards and selling them, I made a new page on Facebook just for them. The birth of Cabro Creations, based on my first email address, it means I can use the same email and it looks intentional. I do get the occasional sale from there but without promotion you don't really get seen.

I promoted it on Google, and I got the occasional contact from there asking what time I open. I have even had a few people applying for a job, and businesses offering to host my staff Christmas party, so it must look good to an outsider.

I still find it ironic that your own family and friends will say how much they like a card you made for them but they are the people least likely to support your small business when you start up. I had so many compliments but no orders ha-ha. But that is ok because I enjoy it so much and plan on expanding to bigger and better things.

I like to crochet, I learnt one night when I was about 16 while staying at my brothers. Angela had left a good housekeeping pull out of how to crochet on the coffee table. There was some wool and a hook there too. I couldn't sleep so decided to have a go, by morning I had learnt the basic steps and made a table doily that had a cone in the middle like a hat lol. But hey I was proud of it and if you stuck an ashtray in the middle no one would ever know !

I gradually improved and managed to make a scarf that was wider at one end than the other, if you can crochet, I KNOW you have been there ha-ha. I soon learnt how to avoid it and started making baby hats, and cardigans for friend's babies. I made a bed jacket for mum because she was going into hospital, I found it in her wardrobe after she died, I broke down and hugged it. I brought it home and it still smells like my mum so I can have a cuddle whenever I want.

I don't know about anyone else but nowadays all the crochet patterns seem to be American, the hook sizes and terminology are all different so I have to translate it in my head as I go " DC, yep that's a treble" that is a whole new skill of its own. You soon get the hang of it once you get going, but if you put it down and come back your brain has to translate it all over again.

I have always enjoyed sewing and made a lot of the children's clothes when they were younger, as they got older, I found I had less and less time but after I left home, I had more time on my hands, I started to make clothes for myself but even now I am not confident enough to sew clothes for others. At first, I was embarrassed to wear them, not because they aren't good enough but if anyone complimented me, I didn't know what to say and would go bright red.

I made a dress, a 50's vintage style dress for a car show. The dress was yellow with vintage cars on it. Perfect for the day, as I walked around everyone said " wow, I love the dress " Or " where did you get the dress?" I was walking around with mum and she told everyone I made it , she was so proud. I kept telling her she didn't have to tell everyone but she just kept on going. After that day I stopped worrying so much and I have made several vintage dresses since then. My next vintage project is a dress and jacket for the steampunk weekend at Whitby. I have the pattern and the fabric I just need to the courage to get the scissors on them.

Everyone assumes that if you have a sewing machine, you do alterations etc. but no that isn't what I do. " Can you take up my curtains ?, I'll pay you obviously". Nope, I am not going down that road !

I discovered making children's and baby clothes again and love it, such tiny things and they come together so easily, making bibs as gifts for new babies, I even discovered the pee pee tee pee, where was that when I had my boys ? I got shot in the eye more than once. Making children's clothing is something I would enjoy but there are so many regulations and safety standard tests it isn't really cost effective. People seem a little snobby sometimes with homemade things, someone once said to me she offered to make baby cardigans for a relative but they declined , then went to Next and Etsy to buy ' hand crafted' baby cardigans for extortionate prices, just for the label inside, which you end up taking out cos it is scratchy for the baby.

I made some t shirts for my grandson, his dad said "Oh I didn't realise you made them they look shop bought, like baby Primark "

" Cheers for that, I thought they were at least on an even par with Baby Boots or Mothercare lol"

Nigel thinks I have too much 'crap'. Yes, I have a craft room and yes it has virtually everything in it, but hang on a minute he bought half the gadgets in there, the new sewing machine, the overlocker and he even bought me a Silhouette cameo cutting machine, it is fab, I can now make shaped cards, gift boxes and other papercrafts. It was a godsend for my wedding. I used it for the invitations, making some of the favours, for decorating the goodie bags and even the light up Gazebos for the table centerpieces.

Someone asked me if I could make some Gazebos for her, after all its only card, yes, it is the best card, it takes 4 sheets for each one, then each one took half a day to put together. Then there is the acetate, and the lights, and the flowers etc. My friend Hannah came to help me and we had a little factory going. Would I want to repeat it for a couple of pounds ? I don't think so.

I can cut heat transfer vinyl and decorate t shirts, baby clothes and make decorative signs, I think it is my all-time favourite toy   ! But again, family and friends will go to Etsy and buy the very things you advertise from someone else, I don't understand why anyone would rather go to a perfect stranger, even risk being conned rather than support a family business. Nigel also bought me a heat press and a mug press; I can virtually make anything now.

So where does he get the 'I have too much crap' from ? I need things to go with the gadgets he buys, I need fabric, card, mugs, t shirts, vinyl...oh yeah and he bought me a sublimation printer so that is a whole new set of 'crap' I need.

Remember I said crafting and buying crafting stuff are 2 different hobbies ? well I rest my case !

And then there is baking, I make some amazing cakes but my decorating leaves a lot to be desired, I am a dab hand with fondant but give me a piping bag and I can make an amazing mess, I really can't control that shit !. I don't fancy going into business making cakes as people really do not want to pay for your time and effort. For example, my wedding cake took 3 full days to make over the space of a week. The ingredients I used were the best, the moulds I bought for the flowers and the time it took to make them. My time alone at a basic £10 and hour would be well over £300 , probably more for someone else because I would be extra vigilant. You need health and safety certificates and not sure having two dogs, even though they are small and don't moult would pass the necessary requirements.

The fact I don't want to bake for a business doesn't mean I don't need the flower moulds, and the dinosaur moulds and the other fancy gadgets that may or may not come in handy

It has been suggested many times I go on Bake off or Sewing bee but I can get pretty frustrated sometimes and swear a lot, that beeping machine would blow up ha-ha

So that's it in a nutshell, there are very few crafts I haven't tried, Incidentally I hate Knitting.

CHAPTER TWELVE: THEY LIVED HAPPILY EVER AFTER

In May 2017 Nigel proposed, we were just laid in bed and he asked if I loved him, I said "of course", he said "oh good cos I got you this" and handed me an engagement ring....such a romantic lol.

To be fair I had planned a trip to Bruges in June for my birthday but it had been cancelled by P and O the month before. Nigel had planned to propose on the trip but when it fell through, he didn't want to wait until my birthday, he is usually so crap at keeping a secret I don't know how he managed it to be honest.

The wedding planning had a few hiccups but we faced them head on. Nigel had got divorced in 2010, his wife divorced him after we had been to California for the Clipper race. My divorce was final a long time before that

Nigel said he would be happy to get married in church if that was what I wanted and at that time we were not sure of the process. I was thrilled, I never really expected that as Nigel isn't a religious person and after all it was a second time around for us both.

I made an appointment to speak to the priest and he said as we had been married before we would have to be granted an Annulment by the Bishop. This meant writing an account of the marriage circumstances and pleading our case. As I had been a victim of domestic violence, I was almost guaranteed it so not to worry.

I was reminded I would be expected to live as a Catholic until we were married, I said I understood and left it at that. When we got outside Nigel asked what he meant by " live as a Catholic" I told him "You know, go to church, go to confession.... Oh, and sleep in separate rooms " I expected him to be disappointed but instead he said " well I am having the front bedroom it has a bigger telly " charming ! I told him not to worry about it anyway I needed something to say at confession before the wedding lol

We both submitted our essays and after a gruelling wait we were granted an annulment. The next step was marriage classes.... yes really! We were both skeptical at first thinking it would be about making babies and teaching grandmothers to suck eggs but it was actually quite a good course. It covered things like finances and the difference between a new relationship and an old relationship. How to work through problems etc. When we got there, we were the oldest couple and the caretakers of the building thought we were leading the group !Anyway, I would definitely recommend it. All the necessary things were completed now and we were ready to go ahead.

I fancied a Christmas wedding but the priest advised me he is busy in December, of course, so we thought maybe the next year, he was "why wait?" October would be good", we informed him Nigel's Ex was getting married in October so wasn't really the best so he said rather than wait let's do it in September and booked a date there and then! We had 6 months to plan a wedding!

We didn't have a huge budget but wanted our family and friends around us, Mum had died the previous year, I was disappointed she wasn't there to see me finally happy , so I really wanted my family to be there.

I decided against having friends as bridesmaids as I have quite a few now and really wanted our Granddaughters to be bridesmaids with Tiffany as my maid of Honour. Both my boys walked me down the Aisle and that was such a special feeling

The wedding was every bit as special as I dreamed of, the service may have been a little long for some but they were warned beforehand and I made activity packs for the children, so no problem really.

I managed to persuade my friends Hannah and Chris to do the readings in Church but struggled to find someone to read the prayers. My friend Vicky offered but she has a naughty streak and I wasn't sure if she was joking. I was also afraid she would swear if she made a mistake. She promised she would rehearse and would do me proud so I gave in in the end.

I had no reason to worry they all did me proud and made no mistakes at all. In fact, Vikki was a total professional. I found out afterwards she had her dress on back to front but didn't know until someone else told her that they had the same dress and it was back to front . She did say she thought it was a bit low and she was aware of her puppies, when she found out she changed it round, I just thought she had a different dress on at the reception to be honest. lol

We booked the wedding for the afternoon so we could just have one reception, inviting everyone we wanted rather than some for the day and some for the night. I made my own invitations and most of the decorations , favours etc. myself. I made some light up Gazebos for the tables and before anyone even sat down, they were putting their names forward to take them home lol

I made the table plan with a Peanut's character theme; each table was named after a character from the show. Ours was obviously the Snoopy table.

I tried to be diplomatic and mixed the tables a little. I had to be careful not to put the naughty people with the nice and easily offended . Some of my work colleagues who are known to be a bit naughty I put with my friends Angela & Kevin and my cousin Sue & hubby Robert who I didn't know that well but I figure if he was Sue's husband, he must be hardy ha-ha, I was not anticipating Vicky doing the YMCA with her legs....in a dress ! Luckily, I was right and it seems my friend's offered entertainment for the whole table.

I even made my own cake which was fab even if I do say so myself. I made a few tester cakes and used my colleagues as Guinea pigs, I had already decided on vanilla for the top to appeal to the boring plain cake eaters but in a kind of aqua rainbow effect. I wanted a fruit cake with Alcohol so it was the middle tier that went for the vote. I preferred the Turkish delight cake but the coconut and Lime one won the vote. My Niece sent me a sugar Snoopy and Belle to feature on it but they were a bit tiny for the top so my trusted cutting machine was used to make a glitter topper and I placed the Snoopy and Belle on there too.

Getting it to the venue was an art in itself. We had to put it in the boot as it was too tall to put on my knee, with an awful lot of sticky tape and bubble wrap we managed to get all three tiers there intact.

Without thinking I posted an image of a cake that had been dropped on Facebook and wrote "Phew, managed to get cake there in one piece" Oh dear, so many people were shocked and thought the pic was our cake, strangely enough they didn't get the joke. I really didn't think they would think it was mine.

When planning the menu for the hot buffet I asked about desserts and maybe a gateau, the hotel wedding planner said it was common to have the wedding cake as dessert now and in their experience sweets and fancy cakes tended to get wasted. They said they would cut it for me and serve it after the statutory cake cutting photos which seemed like a good idea. There was no charge for this so seemed like a great idea. I found out that some venues charge as much as £1 per slice to cut the cake for you , Wow, what a rip off !

They took it into the kitchen and shortly afterwards one of the young caterers came and called me aside with a horrified look on his face, I really thought he had dropped the cake

"Erm, could you please remind me the flavours of the cakes ? "

" Yes of course, the bottom tier is cherry brandy fruit cake, the middle tier is coconut and Lime and the top tier is vanilla"

"oh" "erm"

" Is everything alright"

" I am not sure, is the top supposed to be green ?"

" ha-ha yes, it is in layers of colour to match the wedding theme from cream to aqua"

" Phew we thought it might have gone off and didn't know how to tell you ". Poor kid !

The cake was cut into over 200 portions, and laid out in little rows with Snoopy and Belle placed neatly at the top of the platter, serviettes were supplied in case people preferred to take it home Within about half an hour the cake was gone, I have never been to a wedding where all the cake is eaten. They were like a plague of locusts. I found out after a lot took a piece of each because they couldn't choose . poor Nigel never got any !

As the cake went down, I noticed my Snoopy was missing, I was gutted, turned out one of our friends had taken it as a souvenir not thinking I wanted to keep them so I got it back.

The reception went on until 1 am, when we got up into the Bridal suite, I was exhausted, Nigel put the telly on and was watching Nature watch while I opened the cards . He hasn't let go of the TV remote since ha-ha Not the way I imagined my wedding night to be honest but I was so happy I didn't care.

Our wedding may have been low budget but we had an amazing day and it felt so nice having everyone we wanted there to help us celebrate.

Everyone deserves a happy Ever after and I think I found mine (*except when he hogs the TV remote but I can live with that*)

The start of my Happy Ever After

Whitby Steampunk weekend

About The Author :

Carol Scrimshaw is the youngest of six children and has 3 grown up children from her first marriage. Originally from a council estate in Bradford, she has Now remarried and settled in Kingston upon Hull.

Carol qualified as a registered paediatric nurse after overcoming many obstacles to pursue her career

Now retired and ready to share her story in the hopes of empowering women and girls in the same position to never give up on their dreams.

Printed in Great Britain
by Amazon

86351081R00132